My Horse, My Heart:

The Morgan Horses of the University of Connecticut

By Helen Scanlon

8/30/14
Randy May Memorial

Bob,
Congrats on a
GREAT ride!
Best wishes
and
Happy Trails,

Hel

Cover and book designed by Steve Scanlon, Hampton, Connecticut.
Cover painting, *UC Doc Daniels,* ©2011 Helen Scanlon
Author photograph by Steve Scanlon, *Helen Scanlon with UC Ovation,* 2012

ISBN: 978-0-9894168-0-1

CONTENTS

i   **Dedication**
To Dr. William "Al" Cowan

iv   **Foreword**
John Bennett, Jr., *University of Connecticut Horse Unit Supervisor, American Morgan Horse Association Hall of Fame inductee*

v   **Introduction**
By the Author

PART ONE THE HORSE AND THE HISTORY

2.   **A Schoolteacher and His Horse**
The Origins of the Morgan Breed

5.   **The Horse and the History**
The Morgan Horse and the United States Government Horse Farm

8.   **Sons and Daughters of the Cavalry**
The History of the Morgan Horse at the University of Connecticut

13.   **A Modern-Day War Horse**
UC High Hopes

PART TWO FIRE AND NOBILITY: THE STALLIONS

The Legacy Begins: 1930s

23.   Abbott

1940s-1950s

27.   Canfield
29.   Goldfield
30.   Magellan
32.   Mentor
35.   Panfield

1960s-1970s

37.   The Explorer
38.   Windcrest Don Again
40.   UC Marquis
42.   Ledgemere Bounty
44.   Orcland John Darling
46.   UVM Viking

1980s

48.   UC Ringmaster
60.   Chantwood Command

1990s-2000s

61.   UC Doc Daniels
64.   UC Show Biz
66.   UC Toronado

2000s-2010s

70.   UC Domination
72.   UC Doc Sanchez
74.   UC Mastermind

PART THREE HEART AND SPIRIT: THE MARES

1940s-1960s:

76.	Sheba
78.	Sentana
80.	UC Sensation
81.	UC Melodie
82.	UC Cannie
86.	UC Rhapsody
88.	UC Expectation

1970s-1980s:

89.	UC Taffy
91.	UC Fascination
92.	UC Concertina
94.	UC Lyric
96.	UC Electra
97.	Merwin Black Beauty
98.	UC Sonata
101.	Delmaytion Desire

1990s-2000s:

105.	UC Esther
106.	Song of Courage
107.	UC Aria
109.	UC Ovation
112.	UC Carberry
113.	UC Topaz
114.	UC Hope and Courage
117.	UC Holiday
121.	Salem Sentana

PART FOUR GLIMPSES INTO HISTORY

125. **Glimpses Into History**
We Loved Our Horses

130. **UConn Mare Lines**

131. **America's Horse: The Morgan Horses
Bred at The University of Connecticut**

144. **Acknowledgments**
147. **Author Biography**
149. **Sources**
156. **Illustration Credits**
159. **Index**

DEDICATION

For Dr. William "Al" Allen Cowan
10/4/1920 - 4/4/2009
Professor and Head of the University of
Connecticut Department of Animal Science
from 1952-1985

Dr. William Cowan, 1953

In 2007, I received a phone call.

The caller ID said "Cowan," and I pressed the 'talk' button on my handset, curious.

"Hello?"

"Is this Helen Scanlon, the artist?" said a deep, friendly voice.

"Why yes it is! Who's this?"

"My name is Al Cowan. You painted a portrait of Ringmaster. I need to ask you—what inspired you to paint my horse?"

"Well, he asked me to paint him, and I couldn't say no to the famous UC Ringmaster."

I could hear a smile come through the phone line, and thus started a delightful hour-long conversation with the brilliant Dr. Al Cowan, former head of the Animal Science Department at the University of Connecticut. He would call me several more times that year, and he also sent me literature from UConn's Equine Program, including a breathtaking photo of UC

i

Ringmaster in his heyday, a gold and orange curtain of fall foliage providing a vibrant backdrop.

Dr. Cowan recounted to me the day of UC Ringmaster's birth, the arrival of the stallion Panfield at the University and the loveliness of the broodmares. I wish I had known back then that I would write a book about the magnificent Morgans of UConn—I would have taken some serious notes!

Perhaps Dr. Cowan was asking me to transcribe the history of the Morgan horse at UConn. I feel, in many ways, that he was.

My Horse, My Heart: The Morgan Horses of the University of Connecticut is dedicated to the memory of Dr. William "Al" Allen Cowan. Thank you for the great conversations and for sharing the history with me. You continue to be an inspiration to this writer.

FOREWORD

There are many who do not have a clear understanding of the complexity of the US Government program and its influence on the land grant institutions' Morgan breeding programs.

You will find that Helen Scanlon has made the distinct tie not only between the US Government lines but has covered the occasional outcrosses as well. The UConn program is set apart from other institutions with the student involvement in their light horse program. Helen, in her storytelling, shows just how influential these horses were in the students' lives—whether it was lessons taught or pride in ownership.

The bond between Morgan horses and people continues to be a great one.

It goes without saying that it is a great honor for me to be a part of this history.

~John Bennett, Jr. April 30, 2012
University of Connecticut Horse Unit Supervisor
American Morgan Horse Association Hall of Fame, 2002

INTRODUCTION

My Horse, My Heart

Under a tree, my beloved steed
Earth and roots now hold you near.

Twisted branches scrape the painted sky
With sun to soothe and stars to guide.

My old friend, he is there in the nimbus
Wind shapes his hoof and molds his ear.

I see him in the rays through my window
I hear him in the gust through the flue.

My horse, my heart—he is near.
My horse, my heart—he is here.

-Helen Scanlon, 7/10/11
Inspired by Mentor, government-bred Morgan stallion and
University of Connecticut herd sire, buried in Coventry, Connecticut.

The idea for this book came from a horse.

This horse, a two-time World Champion Morgan stallion, seems to always get what he wants from yours truly. The first time he asked something of me was in 2006.

I was in a UConn Horsebarn stall, helping my friend, Katie, with leg wraps on her polo lesson pony. As I showed Katie how to measure and gauge the wrap on her mount's hind leg, I kept hearing this nickering from a chatty horse three stalls down. It wasn't just a one-time nicker, either. He kept going with a full-blown, animated conversation; talking to anyone who would listen.

"Who the heck is that?" I wondered aloud. I walked down the barn aisle and found the source of the talkfest: UC Ringmaster. He was a big deal when I was student at UConn, winning two World Championships during my time at the school. I recalled reading about him and thinking how cool it was that UConn had such a famous and talented horse. I was about to officially meet him and have my life changed.

And there he was: He was elderly with gray on his temples, but obviously very well-cared for and full of life, acting like a curious and playful yearling. He loved the bustle and activity in the barn; his eyes intently followed the students as they hurried about, dropping brushes and hauling tack.

I walked up to his stall, and he eagerly pressed his muzzle against the iron bars. *Whiffle, whuffle, snuffle, whuff, whuff, wheeeee, snuff,* he said. He seemed quite thrilled that someone had walked over to hear his many stories. We became friends at that moment.

"You certainly have a lot to say," I said to him, instantly smitten.

Whuffle whuff whuff whuff snuffle, he answered.

Ringmaster was so pleased to have someone interested in his oratory that he just kept sharing. This stallion was a bit of a chatterbox, and he charmed me no end.

"Well, isn't that something," I laughed after a particularly animated nickering sequence. "And then what happened?"

Whuff whuffle, he said.

He stuck his nose through the stall opening near his feed tub, and I gently stroked his nostrils and upper lip. He continued to nicker; he was sweet and not at all nippy. He had a gentleman's manner, with upright, perky ears, big eyes, and a dazzling red coat. I had seen many horses in my day, but I had never seen a shade of red this deep and rich on a horse before. It was the color of brewed tea and rust. He was beautiful.

I went home that night and couldn't stop thinking about him. I could hear his incessant snuffling echo in my ears. Never before had I encountered such a casually verbose equine, and I was enthralled.

I decided that I should paint him.

As I picked out the large watercolor leaf for his portrait, I realized that he seemed to ask me to study him and immortalize him with my paintbrush. UC Ringmaster was a natural charmer. He was persuasive but not pushy; a captivating salesman and storyteller—the kind that you trust and like immediately.

Fast forward to 2010. It's 3am, and I am thinking of my old friend, UC Ringmaster. I thought it had been a while since I had seen the great red horse and that I must visit him on my lunch break today. I liked to swing by his barn in order to quiet my brain when the workday got to be overwhelming with endless phone calls, demands and urgencies. He could erase worries and stress with one happy snuffle from his fluttering nostrils. If he was turned out when I visited, I would call out to him, "who's your biggest fan?" and he would hold his head high and trumpet back at me, "Yooouuuuuuu!" He was such a special soul—and I thought—it would be a fun undertaking to write a book about him. Then, another thought: why not a book about all of the stallions? And can't forget those amazing broodmares. I could write it *and* illustrate it!

Then, yet another thought jumped into my mind: what a lot of work! That didn't scare me, however. It invigorated me. I've wanted to write and illustrate horse stories ever since I read *Black Beauty* as a horse-crazy kid.

I made a deal with myself as I lay in bed in the total darkness:

Wait until breakfast. If the idea is still with you then, you must follow through.

Three hours later, with my raisin bran turning to mush in my bowl, the book premise was burning up space in the front of my brain. I now had a promise to keep—to myself, and to UC Ringmaster.

My Horse, My Heart: The Morgan Horses of the University of Connecticut tells the story of the herd stallions and top-producing broodmares from 1931-present, including a riveting tale of the brave gelding UC High Hopes, photographs from the UConn Animal Science Department archives, illustrations and poems by yours truly and a whole bunch of wonderful stories from the people who knew these great horses.

It's been an honor to transcribe this important piece of UConn's history.

~Helen Scanlon
Class of 1994, University of Connecticut College of Liberal Arts and Sciences

Stallion, 2012

PART ONE
The Horse and The History

Because of a Horse

I live today
Because of a horse

My breath flows
My heart beats
My eyes see

Because of a horse

A battle-scarred soldier
Embraced by his family
Rejoicing in his return

And my family carried on

Because of a horse.

~Helen Scanlon 2/8/12

A SCHOOLTEACHER AND HIS HORSE
The Origins of the Morgan Breed

*"This is the story of a common,
ordinary little work horse who turned
out to be the father of a famous family
of American horses."*

~Marguerite Henry, *Justin Morgan Had a Horse*, 1954

In 1789, a dark bay colt named Figure was born in Springfield, Massachusetts.

The colt's story begins with a man, Justin Morgan, a schoolteacher, who was also a talented composer known for his "elegant penmanship." His greatest musical contributions were his renditions of poetry and psalms, known as psalmody. Justin Morgan was a soft-spoken man who held a variety of jobs in his lifetime: tax collector, farmer and "stallioneer." Morgan was an avid horseman, and kept a few mares which he bred to his stallions which stood at stud. Morgan's contribution to the horse world was the small bay colt called Figure, born to one of his mares.

Research has revealed that Figure's sire was most likely a horse by the name of True Briton, a Thoroughbred stallion prized for his conformation and excellence in movement. Figure's dam, Daughter of Diamond, was "...of the Wild-air breed, of middling size, with a heavy chest, of a light bay color, with a bushy mane and tail - the hair on the legs rather long, and a smooth, handsome traveler." She is listed as a half-Arab and traces back to the Godolphin Arabian, through the stallion, Cade.

In 1792, Figure found his way to the schoolteacher as a payment for a debt.

2

It was at this time that Figure began his reputation as the little work horse that could do it all.

Figure was a small stallion, only 14 hands, but his immense strength belied his size. In 1795, Justin Morgan walked Figure from Springfield to Vermont, and when the schoolteacher settled in his new home in the town of Randolph, he rented out the horse to Robert Evans, a local farmer.

Evans used Figure in a variety of farm work: plowing, hauling logs, pulling stone boats and carts. The compact stallion excelled at all of these tasks and never came up lame or winded. When most horses would hang their heads, cock a hind leg and take a much-deserved snooze, Figure still had energy to spare, out-pulling and out-running fresher and younger horses.

In the late 1790s, he raced against the lean and sleek New York-bred horses Sweepstakes and Silvertail in Brookfield, Vermont. Figure won handily and earned the not-too-shabby sum of $50.00, a lot of money for the time. The stretch of Vermont road where the horses tore up the soil, galloping for the finish line, is still called The Morgan Mile.

In 1804, Figure won a pulling bee at General Butler's Tavern in St. Johnsbury, Vermont. The large, draft-style horses were beaten that day by a small horse with a huge heart.

The discerning horse-folk of New England sat up and took notice. Figure was a whirlwind, taking on all-comers with his unassuming looks and small stature. Suddenly, he was the horse everyone wanted in the barn. A durable, sound horse that was an easy-keeper and required minimal oats was a desirable animal for the times.

Figure's popularity skyrocketed and he was offered for stud services in West Hartford, Connecticut; Vermont; Massachusetts; and New Hampshire. Figure was exceedingly prepotent; his foals had his thick neck, strong legs, gentle disposition and compact build. His progeny also inherited his handsomeness with their finely-chiseled heads, full manes and tails, and of course, the huge, liquid eyes.

In 1798, Justin Morgan fell ill, as evidenced by his failing penmanship. When he succumbed to tuberculosis that year, Figure was given his name as an honor. The singing teacher had given New England a fine horse—but even more—he gave the United States of America its very own horse breed.

In 1821, Figure, now widely known as Justin Morgan, was kicked by a pasture mate at Levi Bean Farm in Vermont. Although the 32-year-old stallion was strong, he could not overcome his grave injuries. He died that day, leaving behind a distinguished legacy marked with many successes and seemingly impossible feats of strength and endurance. His gravesite is marked by a humble stone tablet in Tunbridge, Vermont.

One can still drive by the old Bean Farm and see the fields in which the noble Figure spent his final years. The grass in those fields is still grazed on by his descendants.

Today's Morgan horse displays Figure's talent, hardiness, versatility, power and refinement. It is not unusual to see Morgan horses herding cattle, high-stepping in saddleseat classes, pulling carriages, competing in endurance trail rides, sailing over fences and executing flawless dressage tests. The Morgan is a horse that is up to any task at hand.

And, they love people. Morgan horses possess charming and unique personalities that earn them many friends and fans.

The Morgan is truly America's horse.

THE HORSE AND THE HISTORY
The Morgan Horse and the United States Government Horse Farm

"I will give bravery to you through the reins and stirrup leather. There is only forward, now—fearlessly, gracefully, in light. There is Trust."

~ The Morgan Horse

The Morgan horse, the preferred mount of the cavalry, did not shy from gunfire, stayed cool and collected in the face of chaos and was surefooted over uneven terrain. Morgans did not require much fussing and feed, and could carry heavy loads and large men for many miles without tiring. They were also beautiful and flashy, with substance and presence to burn. Many of these horses lost their lives in battle, at times sacrificing themselves for their riders. The bravery and toughness of the cavalry horse is well documented in the annals of history. One of the most famous Morgan war horses was Rienzi, Union General Philip Sheridan's formidable mount. Rienzi was a large, high-spirited black gelding that seemed indestructible: he was shot many times in combat, but always recovered to return to the battlegrounds. Rienzi's bravery was immortalized in the poem "Sheridan's Ride" by Thomas Buchanan Read:

> *...With foam and with dust the black charger was gray;*
> *By the flash of his eye, and his red nostril's play,*
> *He seemed to the whole great army to say:*
> *"I have brought you Sheridan all the way*
> *From Winchester down to save the day."* [excerpt]

The Military reports to the US Government from the Civil War era made particular note of the Morgan's excellence in wartime.

However, by 1905, the Morgan horse was nearly extinct due to the breed's waning popularity. The United States Government answered the urgent call for the preservation of the descendants of the great Figure and established the Vermont Experiment Station in Burlington, Vermont, in the fall of that year. Its sole purpose was to breed, test and care for the Morgan horses for the cavalry and other purposes, and a total of seven mares and two fillies were acquired by the government in June of 1906. The goal of the Vermont Experiment Station was to produce a "true Morgan type," but also to breed for an increase in the size and quality of the breed.

In 1907, Colonel Joseph Battell—the man responsible for creating the first Morgan horse registry—presented to the US Government his 400-acre Weybridge, Vermont horse farm for "the perpetuation and improvement of the Morgan horse." Battell's Bread Loaf Stock farm became known as the United States Morgan Horse Farm, and many believe that Battell's generosity saved the Morgan horse breed from extinction.

At the Government farm, only the best Morgan horses could be used for breeding purposes. A recruitment flyer stated the following standards for mares for their desired herd:

> "Mares: 5 to 8 years old, 15.1 to 15.3 hands tall, weight 1000 to 1150 pounds and sound. Colors preferred: Brown, bay, chestnut and grays, if exceptional individuals."

Stallions were disqualified if they had a "tendency to pace, rack, mix gaits, paddle in front, or sprawl behind." In other words, these horses had to move without flaw, without a hitch, and without hestitation.

The Morgans at the Government farm also had to pass rigorous endurance tests in order to be deemed suitable breeding stock.

Remount stations were also developed to provide horses to U.S. Army units and government-bred stallions were used to improve the local stock. Horses between 4 to 5 years of age were trained and issued to troops—rather than acquiring older, and possibly unsound, horses for the cavalry.

The foundation stallion of the United States Morgan Horse farm was the solid black 14.3 hand stallion, General Gates. General Gates was bred to the bay Saddlebred mare, Mrs. Culvers, and the result was the strong and graceful bay colt, Bennington. Bennington sired Mansfield in 1920, and Mansfield went on to be the United States Morgan Horse Farm's herd sire for the next twenty years. Mansfield possessed a chestnut coat and two perfect white hind socks, a powerful, stout body and smooth gaits much like his sire. Bennington also sired the superb stallion Canfield, who stood at the University of Connecticut in 1948. Canfield in turn sired the Grand Champion stallion, Panfield, an impressive chestnut that stood at the University of Connecticut from 1954-1965.

The University of Connecticut still preserves the integrity of the Government bloodlines. The legacy of Joseph Battell and his generosity lives on in each new foal born in the UConn barns.

SONS AND DAUGHTERS OF THE CAVALRY
The History of the Morgan Horse at the University of Connecticut

"If you're worried, it just means that you need to be shown that there's nothing to worry about."

~The Morgan Horse

The University of Connecticut in the early 1900s was known as the Connecticut Agricultural College, and the school's first equine program bred large and powerful Percheron draft horses. These Percherons provided real horsepower for the college by hauling coal, harrowing fields and clearing hurricane-felled trees from the campus grounds. Students had to learn to care for these horses and, as a result, the academic aspect of horse care was developed at the college. During this time, the school obtained and bred some outstanding individuals, most notably the stallion Dragon, Jr., whose sire was the French-bred Champion, Dragon. In 1917, *The Breeders' Gazette* of Chicago wrote that Dragon, Jr. was "a splendid specimen," "ideal" and "superior." Imposing, with a jet-black coat and weighing over 1,700 pounds, Dragon Jr. was called the "finest Percheron stallion in the East" if not the country. He served as the school's unofficial mascot until his death in 1938. A commemorative stone tablet for the Champion stallion, and a Champion mare, Queen Wolfington, was placed to the east of the horse barn. The horse barn was eventually razed to make room for the Roy E. Jones building, and the stone was moved to a location near the entrance of current horse barns on campus.

By the 1930s, tractors were widely utilized on campus, and the draft horse was used less and less, despite the claim that these horses were "needed more than ever." It was around this time that the first cooperative placement of Morgan stallions from the US Government Horse Farm took place in order to assist in the improvement of the Morgan breed. Dr. Nathan Hale, retired Professor of Animal Science at UConn, recalled to this writer some fascinating details from a 1971 booklet titled "Six Speeches of Walter Stemmons," (Stemmons was the University Editor from 1918 to 1954) transcribed as follows:

> *This speech by Mr. Stemmons was made during a testimonial banquet on February 1, 1942, which was held in honor of Prof. Harry L. Garrigus (Animal Husbandry Professor and first Department Head of Animal Husbandry at the then Connecticut Agricultural College). The paragraph I am referring to appears on page 37: apparently Prof. Garrigus sent a Percheron stallion to the Vermont State Fair, it was sold for $350 and Garrigus was given a Morgan horse "to boot." He also learned that if he could get possession of three registered Morgan mares, the Government would assign a Morgan stallion to the college.*

> *Prof. Garrigus acquired the three Morgan mares as follows: Garrigus purchased one, Director Slate of the college purchased another, and Prof. Garrigus' friend, Mr. William Gumbart of New Haven, purchased the third mare.*

> *The three mares were placed at the college farm, and bred to the Government stallion assigned to the college with their foals becoming property of the school. Thus, the college got into the breeding of Morgan horses with hardly spending a cent.*

> *Prof. Garrigus was a great livestock person and was an exceptional judge of quality horses and cattle.*

In 1931, the Connecticut Agricultural College officially started their light horse program with the Government-bred Morgan stallion, Abbott, and four exceptional mares. The Morgan horse became the cornerstone of the equine program at the Connecticut Agricultural College, providing students with a top-notch education in the training, riding and care of the light horse.

The Connecticut Agricultural College became The Connecticut State College in 1933; and in 1939, it was given its current title of The University of Connecticut.

Four new mares arrive in Storrs, Connecticut, *circa* 1944

In 1950, the demand for Morgan horses declined as the times changed and technology expanded. In response to this waning need, The United States Department of Agriculture (USDA) cut the funding to the US Government Morgan Horse Farm. In 1951, the farm dispersed of their Morgan horses to five Universities—the University of Vermont, the University of Massachusetts, Penn State and the University of Connecticut. UConn received one stallion (Mentor) and four mares at this time. Before the sale, two outstanding mares went to Penn State, Quakerlady and Noontide. Shortly after the dispersal sale, Penn State stopped breeding Morgans, and Dr. Al Cowan, the newly-appointed Department Head of Animal Science at UConn, acquired the mares for UConn's growing Morgan herd. UConn now had the responsibility, and the privilege, to ensure and to perpetuate the noble qualities of the Morgan horse.

It was also at this time that the United States Government Horse Farm was deeded to the University of Vermont, and today the farm welcomes visitors year round. The barns are located about 35 miles from the main campus, and a large statue of the father of the Morgan breed, Figure, watches over the grounds and serves as a reminder of the farm's rich and fascinating history.

For many decades, The University of Connecticut has maintained clear bloodlines tracing back to the Morgan horses bred for the cavalry. These horses are descended from the wartime mounts that were partnered with our men on the battlegrounds. Victories won, but sometimes lost, the Morgan horse was there, his back strong and his legs swift. It is a proud history, a history that you can see in their smooth gaits, muscled flanks and willing dispositions.

The Morgan horse breeding program at the University of Connecticut has felt many an extraordinary hoof beat in its barns and on the expansive clover-dotted fields surrounding them. The bold stallions, the alpha mares, the yearlings in training, the patient lesson horses, the fearless jumpers, the elegant dressage horses, the proud carriage horses, the Champions: they all have their stories and UConn students who loved them and learned from them. Walk through the barns and one can see the trophies and the ribbons, smell the earthy saddle leather and hear the metallic jingle of freshly polished bits and stirrup irons. Barn managers and student workers are quick with a smile as they tack up the lesson horses, fill water buckets and sweep the barn aisles.

Today, the University of Connecticut Morgan horse program still provides an invaluable education for the Animal Science major and the Equine Program student with courses and practicums on breeding, stable management, anatomy, nutrition, equitation, training and genetics. The Morgan horse is revered and loved at the University of Connecticut. It is only fitting for a horse that has given so much to its country.

The blood of the brave steeds that carried men into battle still courses through the veins of the University of Connecticut Morgan horse. The UConn Morgan is truly America's horse, and their bravery, beauty and stamina are legendary.

Morgan horses in Storrs, Connecticut, 2011

As UConn's assistant barn manager, Kathy Pelletier, said,

Once they're gone, that's it. It's like the whales. These are very special horses.

And, if you look into the eyes of a UConn Morgan, you will see a faraway flame, the generations of the lives they touched.

A Modern-Day War Horse
UC High Hopes

"How do you decide to put a young horse down, a horse that had only been under saddle a few months? We had to give him a chance."

-Owner Arlis Bobb on UC High Hopes, "Shoe"

Just how tough is a University of Connecticut-bred Morgan? Does careful breeding with cavalry bloodlines really make for a special kind of horse—a horse that is sturdy, intelligent and kind, with stamina and an incredible sense of self-preservation? The answer is a resounding 'yes.'

The resilient UC High Hopes, a UConn-bred Morgan, exemplifies the true character of the government bloodlines.

The chestnut colt UC High Hopes was born at the University of Connecticut on March 3, 2001. His sire was the bay stallion, UC Doc Daniels, and his dam, UC Hope and Courage, was a daughter of the fiery UC Toronado. UC High Hopes was a handsome sort with a thin white drip of a blaze that followed the contour of his expressive face. He would spin and dance when he was led, and his playfulness earned him the nickname, "Stormin' Norman." He was like the freckled neighborhood boy who would help bring in the groceries, but could accidentally send a baseball crashing through a bay window. He was cute and charming.

As a two-year-old, he caught the eye of trainer Megan Brauch at the UConn horse auction and sale when she was shopping for a suitable horse for her friend and client, Arlis Bobb.

13

Megan had a talent for starting youngsters and had been riding since she was a kid. She knew a special horse was about to enter her life when UC High Hopes stepped into the sales ring that afternoon.

Megan bid on him for a little over Arlis' price because Megan's father insisted she continue bidding even though they were over the limit.

"Arlis won't mind," Megan's father urged. Megan protested, but only a little. She kept bidding. Megan could not ignore UC High Hopes. She would say later that she "fell in love at first sight."

UC High Hopes was sold to Arlis Bobb on April 26, 2003. Arlis now had her young horse to start from the ground up, and she was looking forward to their journey together.

UC High Hopes had a unique spark that indicated spirit, intelligence and tenacity—just like his sire, UC Doc Daniels. Arlis and Megan had no idea how much those qualities would help him in the tumultuous months that would follow his purchase.

UC High Hopes was transported to his new home in Franklin, Connecticut, and soon the little horse was chasing a massive warmblood around the field, asserting his bossiness. He had no fear. His barn name, "Shoe," was inspired by the streak of white on his face that resembled a comet, the Shoemaker-Levy comet, to be exact. It fit him perfectly: he enjoyed being the center of attention, and he had flash in him that could fill the sky if allowed to escape.

Shoe enjoyed his new home, and when Megan began his training, she found him to be an endearing rascal full of smarts and potential. He moved well, he had a good mind and he was a quick study. Once he learned something, he poured his entire being into it and showed his pride like a kid who had just won a spelling bee. Megan knew the "Doc" babies were smart and creative from having trained her own UC Doc Daniels horse, UC Rogue, and she enjoyed the challenge. As their partnership formed, Megan discovered Shoe's steady kindness and willingness to learn. He was a clever little horse with an impish personality, and Megan always looked forward to spending time with him, in and out of the saddle.

Arlis found her ideal equine teacher in Shoe: he managed to get her off his back a couple of times, hence teaching her the importance of a good, balanced seat and a proper position in the saddle. Although animated and precocious, Shoe was never mean-spirited in his lessons. Arlis would always pick herself up, brush the sand from her breeches, and have another go.

But, on a beautiful late Spring day, the young horse's future was dimmed in an instant. In one moment unseen by human eyes, everything changed for Shoe.

Sunday, June 6, 2004, was dry, sunny and pleasant—the sky was rich cerulean without a hint of storm. Under that bright sky, out in the field, Shoe was discovered hunched-up and in extreme pain, a sight no horse owner ever wants to see. Shoe would not be led into the barn without some coercion; this was unusual for the horse that was so willing to please. The vet was summoned.

After an initial examination, the vet surmised that Shoe was "tied up," a term used when a horse has overworked its muscles and toxins have built up in the tissues. Symptoms can include stiff hindquarters, elevated pulse and obvious discomfort.

He was given a painkiller, but he did not improve in an hour. He was responsive and there were no cuts, abrasions or indication of trauma. The vet noted the horse's hind legs were a little swollen and stocked up, but it was "not remarkable." Shoe's abdomen was noted as "tense," and that he was "not excited about walking, but he would." The diagnosis was a case of "tying up and electrolyte disturbance." Instructions were given to walk Shoe twice a day.

Shoe did not improve with time and hand walking; in fact, he got worse, walking more reluctantly each time he was lead. By Wednesday, the vet reevaluated Shoe and x-rayed his entire

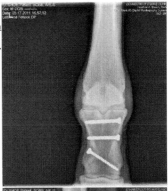
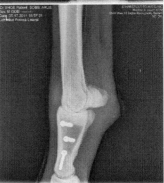
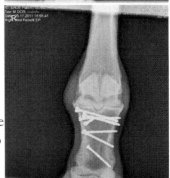
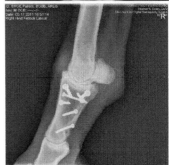

UC High Hopes radiographs, 2011

15

back end. Arlis missed a call back from the vet Thursday night, so she was at the vet's office before it opened on Friday morning, anxious to know what was wrong with her young horse.

The x-ray findings made her heart catch in her throat: *multiple fractures on both hind long pastern bones.*

The x-rays had revealed that the bones were shattered in several places, compressed almost to the coffin bone deep within the hoof itself. His injury was most likely the result of a sliding stop as he cavorted in his paddock.

To put this in perspective: an injury of this magnitude can be catastrophic to a horse. A broken leg usually results in immediate euthanasia, as horses, because of their instincts and anatomy, cannot be relied upon to stay still and quiet in a cast for several weeks as the bones heal. Leg fractures and hoof diseases like laminitis can prove to be tragic for the strongest of horses, and armed even with the best technology, they still present a heartbreaking challenge for vets and farriers.

Now, multiply one shattered leg times two, and you have UC High Hopes, who now seemed aptly named.

Worry and dread consumed Arlis, and she leaned on her friend Megan for support and advice. What to do? Her Stormin' Norman, her Shoe, the copper comet, had so valiantly hidden intense pain and continued to walk on broken bones because his humans had asked him to. Shoe, once a joyful, bright-eyed youngster full of promise, was now dangling between life and death.

As to be expected, the vet had recommended euthanasia. But that just didn't seem right. Shoe was too young and he was a fighter—he had walked on two fractured legs without complaint. He was a tough and stoic character, could he possibly overcome his grave injury?

Arlis and Megan observed Shoe in the indoor arena for hours that day, searching his worried face for a sign, a directive—something that said "give me a chance" or "let me go." Arlis' head swam with questions that had no easy answers:

How do I put a young horse down, one that had been under saddle only a few months?

16

Shoe's eyes still had a glint, that glowing energy befitting a horse named after a comet. In those eyes, they found their answer. Trainer and owner decided that Shoe deserved a chance to put his toughness and positive attitude to the ultimate test, and they decided to send him to Tufts University Large Animal Hospital in Massachusetts in an attempt to save his life. By midday, he had splints on his legs and he was loaded onto a trailer.

When the trailer arrived at Tufts, Shoe backed down the ramp without incident and was brought to a large, deep-bedded stall.

In a separate room, his x-rays were lit up and one vet tech was moved to utter a doom-laden expletive. Here was a real challenge.

The surgery to save Shoe would be extensive—and expensive. While Arlis walked outside to unclutter her mind and get some air, Megan stayed with the vet. With the x-rays still glowing on the monitor, Megan was blunt: *What are his chances?* The vet's response provided the first glint of hope since Shoe had injured himself nearly a week ago. Shoe had quite a few advantages—he was young, small and tough as nails. The vet said he must have "supernatural powers" to be able to walk on two broken legs, so it was worth a shot. He however did warn Arlis of the price of the surgery; it would cost a small mint to fix him, and even then, there was no guarantee he would survive. And, if he did survive, it was doubtful that he would be able to carry a rider again. It did not matter. Shoe had so much life left, and he deserved the chance to go home and live out his days surrounded by his human and equine friends, under a radiant blue sky.

Arlis and Megan gave clear directions to Shoe's medical team: once Shoe was on the table, if they thought he had a reasonably good chance at a happy, pain-free life, then they were to continue with the procedure.

Saturday, June 12, at 8am, and Shoe was on a stainless steel operating table connected to an array of tubes and monitors. His medical team worked on his better leg first, the left, and then had to wake him up, flip him and put him under again to work on the right leg. All in all, Shoe had seven pins inserted into his right hind leg and four in his left. He awoke from the 12-hour procedure in good spirits and a tech noted that despite some pulmonary edema, he "seemed to be feeling fine." Shoe had jumped his first hurdle, but now the real work lay ahead— weeks of hanging in a sling, waiting to heal, with a long list of possible complications that could prove to be life threatening.

To combat depression and boredom, Shoe's recovery stall at Tufts looked like a playpen. Wrapped up in his protective sling, he could reach his milk jug full of rocks and give it vigorous rattle when he wanted a treat. He also had a wiffle bat he could swing and playfully aim for visitors and caregivers. The toys kept his mind busy, but as happy as he was, he could still feel twinges of depression. Two weeks in, heat flared up in his right hind leg. The infection was treated with analgesics and antibiotics and soon he was shaking his rock-filled milk jug again.

Shoe was a cooperative and brave patient, and he took on each challenge with the same positive attitude as when he was working under saddle. He was smart and did not fret in his sling and further injure himself—he seemed to know that the contraption with its many straps and belts was there to help him. The vet techs discovered that their patient curled up his legs and dangled his head when he napped, a scene so precious that a teddy bear and a blanket would have completed the picture. They wanted to take a photo of his snoozing habits to show Arlis, but ultimately decided against it as it might wake him. The young horse needed all of the rest he could get.

After five weeks in a sling having battled depression, boredom and an infection, he was cleared for release from Tufts University Large Animal Hospital on July 21, 2004.

Shoe was moved to a nearby farm where there was the perfect setup for Shoe to have his Tufts-prescribed three weeks of stall rest. Every three days the horse needed to have a multitude of white wraps, padding and tape placed on his hind legs. Curiously, Shoe had developed a fear of anything white. The five weeks of constant dressing changes must have embedded an unpleasant memory in his brain and he could not stand the sight, or smell, of the wraps and padding. His humans attempted to keep the clinical white material out of his sight, and offered comfort and distractions when he became anxious. For all that this strong little horse had to endure thus far, a fear of wraps was all he acquired from his ordeal. His attitude was still stellar, his rascal personality shone through and his ears pricked forward whenever his devoted caregivers were near.

Per vet's orders, he was not allowed to lie down, as he could put stress on his healing hind legs and re-injure himself. Of course, this was easier said than done and his caregivers had the challenging task of ensuring he did not let his legs buckle under him as he tried to make a bed in his stall. They fashioned a surcingle as a sling to hold him up, but Shoe would not have it—he was

18

UC High Hopes ("Shoe") and Megan Brauch, 2012

quite done with slings, thank you. When he felt the straps holding him, he lived up to his first barn name of Stormin' Norman and broke everything in protest. The surcingle snapped, the halter ripped off his face and he even shattered light bulbs above his head in his quest to be free. Exhausted, his humans relented. The surcingle was removed, and Shoe went to work very carefully folding his legs and plopping his body into the deep bed of wood

19

shavings. He let out a blissful and contented sigh. For over five weeks of being suspended in a sling, Shoe was finally able to relax. Shoe's sense of self-preservation prevailed, and when he stood up, he was mindful of his legs and he carefully placed them under his body so he did not hurt himself and undo hours of surgery and weeks of convalescence.

It had been weeks at this point, and Shoe was growing impatient and he wanted to play. He started feeling good. *Really* good. He felt the need to flare his nostrils, fill his lungs, kick up clods of earth and fly. On September 21, 2004, his medical team said that he could be hand-walked twice a day. Not quite the complete freedom he desired, but it was close.

For his exercise sessions, Shoe had a halter slipped over his head and two chain leads affixed over his nose, with a handler on each shank. Shoe was like caged lightning as he danced, snorted and pawed the ground under his feet. The chains on his nose and chin reminded him to contain his energy as he was still in danger of re-injury. Shoe, true to his intelligence, never tested his handlers and did not try to break free, but his message was clear: let me *run*.

In October, Shoe was moved to a farm in Columbia, Connecticut, where he could have an ideal small turnout to stretch his legs and taste real freedom. It was around this time Megan began working him again. She long-lined him and helped him to re-learn to pick up his hind feet. His hooves were narrow from the months of being wrapped up and constricted, and he liked to lean on Megan when she handled them. Shoe trusted his trainer and soon learned that his once-injured hind feet could carry him without the slightest twinge of pain.

Although Shoe was progressing well, the prognosis was still that he would be a pasture buddy, and not a riding horse. It was a full year before Megan decided to get on his back and test that prognosis. Shoe's mind was clear and sharp, and he wanted a job.

For his first work since the accident, Shoe trotted stiffly, but his walk was fluid and forward, a promising sign. With more exercise, his joints warmed up, and soon he was moving freely with a rider astride him. Megan had him trot over poles to encourage flexion, keen to Shoe's body language. He never indicated pain and he enjoyed being active, so Megan continued his lessons. She noticed his canter felt tight—and he would occasionally kick out in what Megan called "horse frustration." He desperately wanted to get it right: the work ethic was still there, as strong as ever. He was a true war horse: he was strong and he was determined.

With regular work, Megan decided he was well enough to try a couple of schooling shows. The story of the 'bionic super pony' was making the rounds. Could it be that this little copper-colored horse broke both hind legs and not only healed, but was now getting a high score on a dressage test?

At one show, a perceptive judge who did not know Shoe's story made the remark that the handsome Morgan gelding seemed "a little stiff behind" during his dressage test.

Megan could only laugh a little and say, "You have *no* idea."

Stormin' Norman, Shoe, UC High Hopes, now enjoys the normal life of a horse. He struts around the turnout like he owns it, shoves his feed tub at people demanding treats and he carried Megan in not one, but three, Rides for the Cure, an eight mile trail ride to benefit the Komen Foundation. Their story, along with a beautiful photograph of horse and trainer, was featured in Women's Health magazine.

In August 2010, Megan Brauch and UC High Hopes were High Point Dressage Champions at the Randy May Memorial Schooling show at Little Divide Farm in Mansfield Center, Connecticut. Shoe moved obediently and smoothly, flicking his ears back and forth as he listened to Megan's hand, leg and seat cues.

The team presented a harmonious picture of teamwork and friendship.

UC High Hopes, Shoe, with his eyes full of trust and playfulness, has endeared himself to all who have had the honor of meeting him.

"Oh, *this* is the horse," they say.

"So, that's the Super Pony!"

Shoe proved that pain and fear can be overcome, and that hope can live on in even the direst of circumstances. Shoe is a survivor.

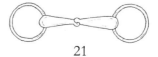

PART TWO
Fire and Nobility: The Stallions

My Teacher

I knew the shape of your kind face
Golden and noble, painted with blaze.

Breezing over the russet-painted earth
We were joined by bridle, bit and girth.

~Helen Scanlon 8/28/11

The Legacy Begins: 1930s

Abbott
Monterey [sire]-Kylona [dam]
Born: 1930
University of Connecticut Herd Sire from 1931-1935

He is well known to Connecticut horse lovers, and the influence he has had upon improving the horses of the state is remarkable. ~1936 *Block and Bridle Program*

Abbott was a dark chestnut, sturdy of build and stout of heart. Professor Harry Garrigus acquired him for the then Connecticut Agricultural College from the Government Farm as their first Morgan herd sire in 1931. He was broken to saddle by student Howard Raven, and the deep-red stallion produced the mares Joyous and Phillipa during his time at the school. Joyous was a beautiful and uniquely colored mare: she was listed as "minimal sabino" and possessed a golden bay coat with a startling blaze that covered both nostrils.

Phillipa, born in 1933, was a feminine chestnut mare with exceptional athleticism. She was a good size, hitting the tape at 15.1 hands, and she was used heavily in class work and in the school's breeding program. She was a star in the student and open horse shows at UConn, finishing in the ribbons most of the time. Phillipa was one of the first Morgan broodmares at UConn, producing UC Mayphil and UC Cannie, two excellent mares in their own right. Phillipa died at 24.

Abbott was a gorgeous beast, with an animated, expressive face highlighted with a large star on his forehead and a swipe of white on his muzzle. His large eyes would follow and observe with white-rimmed intensity.

Abbott lived at the University of Massachusetts after his breeding career at

Abbott, *circa* 1932

UConn came to a close. There, a student by the name of Al Cowan rode him regularly.

Al Cowan, future Head of the Animal Science Department at UConn, enjoyed riding the stallion on brisk jaunts around the UMass campus. One day, he left his shirt in a hay field, disposed of when the sun's midday heat became oppressive. Later that day, upon discovering he had left his shirt in the field, Al swung a leg over Abbott's back and rode out to fetch his forgotten garment. In the near distance, young Al spotted a pretty girl out for a walk. He smiled broadly and waved to the girl, feeling confident and brave on his noble steed. Just when he was sure the young woman would be duly impressed by his riding prowess, Abbott made a hard, humbling turn to the left, leaving Al on his back in the middle of the Amherst hay field. Indifferent and unimpressed, the pretty lass walked on.

Al picked himself up, plucked the dried grass from his hair and checked his pride. His face felt flushed and red. He gazed up at his horse, and the animal regarded him calmly.

He could swear Abbott was smiling.

A few years and a graduate degree later, Al Cowan was appointed the Head of the Animal Science Department at UConn. He held that title for over thirty years.

In a 1997 panel discussion for the American Morgan Horse Association in Boston, Massachusetts, Dr. Al Cowan stated this about his old friend, Abbott:

> *As an undergraduate at UMass in the years 1938-1942, I rode the Morgan stallion, Abbott, a great deal. I liked him. He sold me on his kind.*

And so began the incredible legacy of fine UConn Morgan horses bred under the expert direction of Dr. Al Cowan. We have Abbott to thank for lighting the fire in Al Cowan's heart, even if he did dump him in a hay field.

Abbott's personality and intelligence made him many friends, and Howard Raven, '33—who went on to be a well-respected veterinarian in Fairfield, Connecticut—wrote this letter to UConn, and it was published in a 1962 Block and Bridle program under the heading "Stallion Memories":

> *I am enclosing a review from 1938. Please add it to your collection if you don't already have it, but I would appreciate its return if you have a duplicate as it has a very sentimental value to me.*
>
> *You see—it was sent to me by Professor Harry Garrigus in 1938 because the cover page was of "Abbott"—the first Morgan sire at the then Conn. Agricultural College.*
>
> *At the wish of not boring you I'll give you a little history.*
>
> *Abbott, along with three Morgan mares were the first Morgans brought to the college in the late fall of 1931. I was given the great pleasure and privilege of breaking and training him.*
>
> *With the help of Andy Carter (then in charge of the horse barn) I worked on him for a year and a half and had many pleasurable hours riding over the hills surrounding Storrs.*
>
> *I might add that he was without a doubt the smartest and best dispositioned horse I have ever encountered---and that is a few, as my practice today is quite extensively a horse practice.*

It is April, and the nights are still somewhat frigid—a hint of winter permeates the air. A broodmare shuffles in her stall, and she groans as she lies down in the deep straw. The mare gives birth to a dark colt with two white swirls on his face and a mischievous twinkle in his intelligent eye. Steam rises from the colt's flanks as he finds his legs under him, eventually standing to nurse. The mare nickers as she licks her foal's damp coat, each touch deepening the bond between them. In that barn, in the early spring morning, the spirit of the magnificent chestnut stallion known as Abbott lives on.

Canfield

Bennington-Artemisia
Born: 1932
University of Connecticut Herd Sire from 1942-1948

Royally bred....With very limited opportunities, Canfield has proved himself a real sire. ~1942 *UConn Block and Bridle Program*

A handsome, deep chestnut stallion with a wide blaze and bright eye, Canfield was herd stallion at UConn for six years. A full brother to Mansfield, chief sire at the Government Horse Farm, he made two trips to the college—the first time as a young horse and the second time in 1946 to assume stud duties after the death of Goldfield who had passed on two years previously.

Around the time of his career at University, the UConn Morgan horses were used more as saddle horses. Canfield was used successfully in the riding program, and photos from that era show him proudly carrying students on his broad back. He had a solid build with a pronounced crest, and he possessed a regal air that commanded reverance.

His show accomplishments include winning the Rafferty Challenge for Morgans three years in a row, and, as a 1942 Block and Bridle program

Bessie Amston rides Canfield, 1941

27

states, "in a limited Morgan class he has never been defeated."

He was a stallion that was impressive and stately, and he transmitted his outstanding qualities to his offspring to a great degree. Some of his most famous progeny include Bennfield (who went on to sire the famous Bennfield's Ace), Panfield and the much-loved mare, Cannie.

Canfield, 2012

Goldfield

Mansfield-Juno
Born: 1936
University of Connecticut Herd Sire from 1941-1944

[The Morgan horses at UConn] are living up to the standards of their breed—gentleness, stamina, style and smooth gaits…. Heading the Morgan breeding program is Goldfield. ~1943 UConn Block and Bridle Program

Goldfield was bred at the Government Farm to the lead herd stallion, Mansfield, out of the bay mare, Juno. Goldfield was a stunning chestnut colt with a powerful shoulder and a majestic head. He'd sired nearly the entire 1942 Government Farm foal crop before arriving at UConn.

He showed well at the annual Morgan horse show in Woodstock, Vermont, taking third place in both the Morgan stallion and Get of Sire classes. A 1943 photograph of Goldfield carrying a UConn student clearly shows his nobility, refinement and strength. His head is lofty and his legs are positioned in a perfect square halt. The student astride him wears a beaming smile on her face; a clear spring sky and a lush hay field frame their pose. It depicts a wonderful moment in time for the young student and the Morgan stallion—a memory that no doubt stayed fresh for that student for many years. UConn was enthusiastic to have the mighty Goldfield as a herd sire, and many mourned him when his life was cut tragically short by a blood clot in 1944. He sired many successful progeny— amongst the standouts were Mentor and Magellan, both of whom stood at UConn as herd stallions. His death was a huge loss to the Morgan horse world; Goldfield had so much left to do. However, his illustrious,

Helen Carter on Goldfield, 1943

government-bred blood is apparent in many modern-day Morgan horses. Goldfield was a grand horse and he is not forgotten.

Magellan

Goldfield-Topaz
Born: 1942
University of Connecticut Herd Sire from 1944-1946

Magellan came to UConn in 1944 to replace Goldfield as herd stallion from 1944-1946. A chestnut with a corn-silk mane and wisps of dapples on his sides and flanks, Magellan was bred by the Government Farm in 1942. His stay at UConn was a short, but influential one: during his two years he sired Pennsy, Penny Royal, Royalanne and Mayphil.

In 1947, Magellan was sold to the Chinese Nationalist government as a military mount. Major General P.C. Tsui, Deputy Chief of the Horse Administration Bureau, Ministry of National Defense, China sent a letter to F.B. Hills, Secretary of The Morgan Horse Club, detailing the arrival of Morgan horses shipped to China. The following is an excerpt of Tsui's letter, dated December 31, 1947:

> We left United States October 1 and landed at Shanghai October 22. Bad storms gave us a send-off in the Eastern Pacific and welcomed us in the Western Pacific. The horses stabled on board took many a bath. One Quarter mare aborted but the others stood the trip comfortably.
> The horses will remain at Shanghai until the end of January when they will be removed to the Northwest and the Southwest in the interior of China by airplane. Magellan 8625 from the U.S. Morgan horse farm will be senior stallion at the Military Min-Sian Stud in Kanush Province.
> .... When we arrived at Nanking, we had a conference. It was attended by all the leaders of the Horse Administration Units....When they later went to Shanghai with me they all liked the Morgans. After a critical examination, they agreed they liked best Magellan and Red Rockwood.
> Many students of the Agriculture School, headed by their professor, came to look at the horses. I introduced them to the story and the best points of the Morgan horses. You and the members of the Morgan Horse Club will be most happy to know that the first Morgan horses to come to China made a fine impression.
> ....Maj. Gen. S.C. Wang, the Chief of Min-Sian Stud, (is) the new master of Magellan. Gen. Wang, one of the most experienced horsemen in China; was most delighted with Magellan.

Magellan, strong and surefooted, was last seen serving in the Korean War with a Communist Chinese officer astride him, most likely Major General S.C. Wang.

The fate of the brave stallion remains a mystery, but one can imagine he held his head high and fearlessly carried his rider through smoke and artillery fire.

Such is the nature of the cavalry Morgan, and it lives on in the Morgans of the University of Connecticut. In their eyes you can still see the reflection of the cannon fire of long ago.

Magellan, *circa* 1945

Mentor

Goldfield-Fairytop
Born: 1942
University of Connecticut Herd Sire from 1951-1962

We are indeed proud to have such an animal in our horse barn.
~1951 University of Connecticut Block and Bridle program

Figure, the original Morgan, was a prodigious stallion, passing on his sturdy conformation, stamina and handsome looks to his progeny. In 1942, Figure seemed to be born again in a colt by the stallion Goldfield out of the mare Fairytop.

This was Mentor.

Mentor, bred by the Government Farm, arrived at UConn in 1951 when the Government herd was dispersed. In addition to Mentor, UConn was given the mares Penny, Pennsy, Quotation and Sheba.

Mentor was a bit of a sensation when he arrived at UConn. He was a three-time National Champion and was considered by many horsemen of the time as possessing the "best form towards Morgan type in the world today." He was touted as "the last hope of the Morgans," to pass on his strength, brilliance and near-perfect classic Morgan conformation to the UConn herd and beyond. Mentor was a stunning equine specimen: his neck was thick with a clean throatlatch, his shoulder was sloping and powerful and his legs were sound and strong as steel. Highly intelligent and stately with a rich, dark chestnut coat, Mentor sired many foals during his time at UConn, including Quakerlady, Riviera, UC Highlife and UC Senator.

Mentor left UConn in 1962 when he was sold to Mr. William Glenney of Coventry, Connecticut. Mentor was known to be gentle and kind in his golden years, and could sometimes be seen giving toboggan rides to delighted children across snow-covered fields. William Glenney loved his horse and provided the Champion with a comfortable retirement.

Mentor breathed his last at age 27. The stallion's body forever rests in that quiet, verdant land, less than twenty minutes away from the University where he left his proud hoofprints.

Mentor at The Big E, 1956

Afterword

In my research for this book, I received an e-mail that opened with these lines:

> *I owned a beautiful gelding who came by way of the University of Connecticut breeding program. In 1963, my father bought Conquistador, sired by Mentor out of UC Pandora...*

33

It is a rare and beautiful thing when research leads directly to the people who were touched by these Morgan horses of long ago. Intrigued, I asked the author of the e-mail to tell me more. Much to my delight, I received a response almost immediately. The memories, including a scan of a faded black-and-white photo of UC Conquistador, filled my e-mail inbox.

In 1963, a 13-year-old girl by the name of Pamela was given the most wonderful gift a horse-crazy kid could ask for: a golden-maned Morgan horse gelding. Conquistador was, according to Pamela, "a giant in heart and personality." Pamela rode him saddleseat and showed in pleasure, equitation, in-hand and driving. "Conky" won Reserve Champion for in-hand at the St. Jude's horse show, where Pamela proudly recalls riding in the horse van with her winner, his head poking out the window as they journeyed home exhausted, proud and happy. Pamela clearly remembers her horse show days with her chestnut gelding. She recalls the four leaf clovers her father picked for her to keep in her pocket and the blue carnations her mother stuck in her lapel, and her horse, ever steady and true, winning the ribbons and cantering effortlessly when all the other horses in the ring fussed and disobeyed. Conquistador stayed with Pamela until he was 16, and it is easy to see her transform into that proud 13-year-old girl as she writes about her horse:

> I hope you can tell that this 64-year-old lady back in the day was taken over by a marvelous fellow called "Conquistador."

The Morgans of UConn are so much more than the herd stallions and the broodmares. They are the foals that grow up to be Champions, teachers, partners and best friends. They are the horses that can elicit the joy of younger days, trotting in a dusty show ring under a summer sun, and walking out with a ribbon clipped to the bridle. There are trunkfuls of those ribbons, somewhere, each one holding a proud memory of that special horse: the UConn-bred Morgan.

Panfield

Canfield-Karina
Born: 1945
University of Connecticut Herd Sire from 1954 -1965

> *I had always admired Panfield and wanted to use him when I came to Connecticut.* ~Dr. Al Cowan (from *Who's Who in New England Morgandom, New England Morgan Horse Association*)

Correct. Stunning. Beautiful. Moved as if gliding across a ballroom. This was Panfield.

Panfield, a handsome chestnut with a wheat-colored mane and tail, was bred by the Government Farm in 1945. He was a National Champion in 1949, defeating the formidable competition of Upwey Ben Don, Mentor and Orland Leader, in that order.

Dr. Al Cowan had admired Panfield from the moment he saw him as a young stallion at UMass, where Cowan had been a faculty member. The Government Farm had loaned Panfield to the school for a year, and when the dispersal was imminent in 1951, Cowan wanted to retain Panfield for the UMass breeding program. The USDA had other plans, however. They featured the National Champion as senior stallion in the sale.

Panfield was sold to an impressed Locke Theis of Kansas. The long trip to the Midwest was a hard one for the stallion—Panfield had broken his knee in the railroad car and as a result could no longer be ridden or driven. His show career was cut short, but he was still a magnificent stallion, and his breeding future was sure.

Panfield remained in the front of Cowan's mind when he accepted his new position at UConn in 1952. Enter J. Cecil Ferguson of Broadwall Farm in Greenfield, Rhode Island: Ferguson bought a large group of Morgans from Theis in the middle of a terrible drought, and Cowan assisted in the purchase by offering his expert eye. Of course, he encouraged Ferguson to purchase his favorite, Panfield. Ferguson trusted his good friend, and bought the stallion without a second thought.

In 1954, Ferguson brought some mares to UConn, and he included Panfield in the deal, knowing how much his friend Cowan revered the majestic blond stallion. He joined Mentor in herd stallion duties, and in doing so, he made UConn the only Morgan breeding operation in the country to make the claim of having two National Champion stallions in their barns.

For many years, Cowan was vocal with his gratitude for the generosity of his friend, "Fergie." Panfield was used extensively at UConn and, as Al Cowan stated, it was Panfield that made his presence particularly felt in the breeding program. His daughters UC Melodie, UC Rhapsody and UC Sensation shone as stellar broodmares and passed their exceptional qualities on to their foals.

Panfield was sold in 1965 to Phil Beckley of Oregon, and although he was twenty years old, he was still a fertile stallion and continued siring outstanding foals.

The mighty, big-hearted stallion died on his 29th birthday after sustaining a broken leg due to a kick from a mare. A tribute with a presentation featuring eleven of his sons and daughters, including a weanling, was paid to him at the Oregon Morgan Horse Show on June 30, 1974. The Morgan Horse Magazine featured an article on him in their October, 1974 issue, titled, "Panfield: 1945-1974—One of the Last of the Old-Timers," written by Leo Beckley.

He sired a total of 131 registered foals during his lifetime.

Panfield added flash with substance to the UConn Morgan program and his influence is still felt many generations later. He was a stallion of fantasy. But, he lived. He was real.

And, somewhere, a golden Morgan horse dances over a lush, open field, his ivory mane reflecting the rays of the summer sun. The stallion of fantasy is still with us, his bloodlines strong and true.

Panfield, *circa* 1950

The Explorer

Senator Graham-Flyette
Born: 1958
University of Connecticut Herd Sire from 1961-1962

The Explorer was a chestnut stallion with a light-gold mane and tail that demonstrated classic Morgan horse conformation and beauty. After he won second place in the stallion foal Morgan Futurity class at the Illinois State fair in 1958, he was purchased by Richard and Irene Greenwalt.

Animal Science professor John Kays purchased The Explorer for UConn in 1959. The stallion was used in limited service at UConn, but he produced such outstanding individuals as UC Exhilaration, UC Expectation, UC Ecstasy, UC Exploration and UC Expression. His daughter, UC Expectation, became a top-producing broodmare for the University. In 1961, Explorer was an established sire and was bred to nearly all of the UConn broodmares. He was gelded shortly thereafter and was used in the riding program.

As he aged, he became, according to one student, "a bit of a lovable curmudgeon," but always retained a gentleman's way about him. The Explorer was a fine teacher, and many UConn alumni recall his endearing grouch personality with fondness.

Windcrest Don Again

Upwey Ben Don-Mademoiselle of Windcrest
Born: 1962
University of Connecticut Herd Sire from 1963-1973

We have a flashy newcomer at the barn by the name of Windcrest Don Again…Come on down and look this yearling over. ~1963 UConn Block and Bridle Program

In 1962, Dr. Al Cowan was interested in acquiring new blood for the UConn herd, and set out on a quest to find a stallion with an outstanding pedigree. He contacted Ted Davis of Wind-Crest Farms in Vermont, knowing that he had the celebrated stallion, Upwey Ben Don, as the farm's herd sire. Dr. Cowan explained to Davis that he didn't have a large budget with which to buy a good breeding stallion, so Davis offered Cowan the pick of any colt on the farm for $500. After inspecting the field of colts, Dr. Al Cowan spotted a stunning dark bay youngster playing alongside his dam and could see a future Champion stallion in the long-legged foal. For that mere few hundred dollars, UConn had its future herd stallion. The youngster was given the lyrical name of Windcrest Don Again by Cowan and Davis, and the colt was spectacular: otherworldly beautiful, even-tempered and tractable. Alumni from that time recalled him as being a gentleman of the highest order.

Upwey Ben Don came to Wind-Crest Farm much like his son Windcrest Don Again came to UConn: Ted Davis spotted Upwey Ben Don as a colt and couldn't get him out of his mind. He couldn't afford him at the time he first saw him, funds were tight because of World War II—but he kept the colt on his radar. When Davis finally set out to buy his future herd stallion he braved a massive New York snowstorm to retrieve him, his daughters Patty and Helen in tow. When Upwey Ben Don trotted down a snow-covered driveway that day, all Davis could think was "if he could trot like that in this weather, imagine what he could do in a show ring." He possessed a trot that floated like a leaf in a brook.

In his day, Upwey Ben Don could induce nervous, awestruck butterflies in the guts of his horse and human competition. The stallion could practically just show up, strut off the trailer and grab all the ribbons and trophies.

In addition to his show ring successes, Upwey Ben Don was a five-time winner of the Get-of-Sire class at the National Morgan Horse show. He was an immortal sire and performance horse, and mention of him still inspires animated conversation in Morgan horse circles.

Windcrest Don Again sired many incredible Morgans for the UConn herd, including UC Donation, UC Fascination, UC Marquis (also a UConn herd sire), UC Dark Shadow, UC Prima Dona, UC Flirtation (dam of World Champion UC Royal Dutchess) and UC Lyric (dam of two-time World Champion and UConn herd stallion, UC Ringmaster).

The Upwey Ben Don qualities, combined with the government bloodlines, created a Morgan horse that had it all: correct and beautiful gaits, flawless conformation, stamina, longevity, superstar presence, kind temperament, willing attitude and unparalleled hardiness.

Windcrest Don Again was a horse that allowed many to be a part of living, breathing history. His contributions to the UConn herd were far-reaching and significant.

Not bad for a $500 colt.

Windcrest Don Again, 2012

UC Marquis

Windcrest Don Again-UC Cannie
Born: 1967
University of Connecticut Herd Sire from 1973-1976

The newcomer who this year took the Eastern circuit by storm.
~1978 UConn Block and Bridle Program

UConn produced some astounding Morgan horses by crossing the show-ready beauty and tractable personalities of the Ben Don line with the durability and textbook correctness of the Government line. One such mating produced the striking bay stallion, UC Marquis. His sire was Windcrest Don Again, the dark bay son of the multi-Champion Upwey Ben Don. His dam was UC Cannie, the kind-hearted mare with a strong Government-influenced pedigree.

UC Marquis was a vision with his sleek coat and high head carriage with power and energy to spare. Trainer Bob Brooks said this of UC Marquis:

Marquis was a lot of horse, proud and full of testosterone. He was all stallion.

Marquis was a cover boy for the 1970 *UConn Block and Bridle Program*, and the black and white photo depicts the stallion in a moment of regal repose—his ears up, his nostrils open, taking in the air. His black foretop is gently pushed to the side and kept in place by a polished brow band. He fills the program cover with his confident gaze—this is what writer John Taintor Foote meant by "the look of eagles." He began his breeding career at UConn in 1971.

Marquis was a dynamic horse that loved to work, and he was happiest when he had a regular schedule to keep him centered, fit and focused. In 1975-76, two students, Amy LaMotte and Sue Valley, both experienced saddleseat riders, started training Marquis as a Park Morgan. Amy and Sue also cross-trained him in harness, and Marquis relished the attention and did well. The students were mindful to balance his work schedule with the occasional trail ride, and Marquis enjoyed the nature excursions immensely. Marquis was a brilliant mover, propelling his whole being forward in his work, commanding attention from all eyes. The handsome, gossamer-gaited stallion acquired an enthusiastic fan base amongst the students at the barn.

His early training complemented his work ethic and he soon became a

40

superstar, winning Grand Champion Stallion at the Connecticut All-Morgan Show and the Granite State Morgan Horse Show, Champion Park Harness at the Granite State Morgan Horse show— and he was second in the Five and Over Stallions at the prestigious New England Regional Championship show. He was shown by Bob Brooks in these multiple wins. His successful progeny include Intrepid Sovereign (two-time World Champion in the Classic Pleasure Division), and the UConn-bred UC Electra and UC Spicy Lass.

He was sold to Arthur Perry, Jr. of Intrepid Farm in California, where he continued to delight and thrill the Morgan horse world in the Park Harness classes. He also appeared several times in the Tournament of Roses Parade in Pasadena, California.

He was every bit the bold, aristocratic Morgan stallion.

UC Marquis, 1970

Ledgemere Bounty

UVM Cantor-Naive
Born: 1967
University of Connecticut Herd Sire from 1975-1977

A little stallion with the big moves.

Patti Brooks, Morgan breeder, rider and author, was sold on the Morgan breed when she was 13 years old. Her first horse, Chief, was an army mount with a government brand on his neck. When she wrote to Washington and tracked down his records, she discovered he was a Morgan bred at a remount station in Texas. Chief won Patti's heart, and she became a Morgan horse enthusiast from the moment that they forged their friendship.

Patti's high school graduation present was a yearling Morgan filly, UVM Charm. Patti's five siblings were given cars when they graduated, but she insisted on a horse. The young Patti was quite outspoken about her position to utilize horses instead of automobiles; she resisted the use of the four-wheeled mode of transportation. Instead, she embraced the life of a rider and preferred the view of the world from a saddle. Patti found Ledgemere Bounty by way of another son of UVM Cantor and Naive, UVM Jim Dandy. Jim Dandy was a fine colt with correct gaits and a stellar disposition, but sadly, the youngster died during castration surgery. Patti, seeking to find a colt with Jim Dandy's brand of brilliance, set out to own another son of UVM Cantor and Naive.

In 1969, Patti acquired the two-year-old chestnut colt, Ledgemere Bounty—a full brother to UVM Jim Dandy. He showed excellence early on.

Ledgemere Bounty, "Bounty,'" was a small horse with big action. He carried his neck more forward than upright, yet he maintained a large and light-stepping motion, and he was undefeated in the show ring in the Park Harness division. However, as a three-year-old, Bounty was shown only once under saddle before he mysteriously lost sight in one of his eyes. The blindness halted a promising show career for the young stallion, but it marked the beginning of a successful breeding career. Dr. Al Cowan was impressed with the unconquered stallion, and he contacted Patti's husband, Bob Brooks, to discuss Bounty becoming a UConn herd sire. A nice horse that was easy to handle, Bounty was a senior stallion for UConn from 1975-1977.

Bounty's blind eye was not a genetic fault, and he sired many talented and handsome progeny for UConn, including UC Harvestor, UC Tip Top, UC Topaz and UC Sonata.

Bounty was a little stallion, but he possessed a distinctive and powerful voice. Patti described his neigh as a "loud roar that sounded like it came out of a 17-hand warmblood."

He also had a big personality. Patti recalls the time Bounty was turned out in a paddock next to the much larger stallion, Serenity March Time. The stallions were separated by a wood and electric fence barrier, but that did not stop Bounty from reaching through the slats and grabbing the bewildered Serenity March Time by his abundant foretop. Patti concluded that Bounty saw the other stallion's flowing hairdo, and he just couldn't resist snagging it and taking him for a little drag. Both stallions were unharmed in the incident, and it further demonstrated just how unfazed Bounty was by horses bigger than he.

When Ledgemere Bounty concluded his stud duties for UConn, he continued to sire beautiful Morgan horses that brought many ribbons and trophies to their proud owners. The little chestnut stallion with the big heart left his proud mark on the Morgan horse world.

The Ledgemere Bounty influence is still seen in the UConn herd today. Perhaps, if we listen closely, we can still hear the echoes of his clamorous trumpeting from one of his children.

Ledgemere Bounty, 2012

43

Orcland John Darling

Ulendon-Anna Darling
Born: 1965
University of Connecticut Herd Sire, 1974

My own favorite memories of John Darling have nothing to do with his show ring or breeding achievements. During his quiet days of retirement, there were long, quiet rides on the fields and trails of West Newbury, Mass. I like to think he enjoyed them, too. ~Bill Crawford, "I Lost a Good Friend," 1978 *Morgan Horse Magazine.*

Orcland John Darling was UConn herd stallion in the early 70s, leased from Dr. and Mrs. Lyman Orcutt of Orcland Farms, West Newbury, Massachusetts. He was a sharp, well-proportioned stallion—he had a rich chestnut coat with two perfect white hind socks and a vast, dramatic star between his eyes. Under the joint ownership of Marlo Farms and Orcland Farms, he was successfully shown as a yearling in Colorado, trained by Martin Cockriel stables. Orcland John Darling was a gifted performer, chalking up many wins in Harness, In-Hand and under saddle including first in Park Horse in Harness and Combination Park, and a second in Park Horse Under Saddle at the Uvada All Morgan Horse Show in Las Vegas, Nevada. He was crowned the 1970 American Horse Show Association Morgan Horse of the Year, Park Division.

He returned to Massachusetts in 1970 to take over stud duties from his recently deceased full brother, the 1963 National Champion, Orcland Don Darling.

John and Don's sire, the superb Ulendon, died the year Orcland John Darling was born, leaving a proud legacy of outstanding offspring. Their dam, Anna Darling, foaled three colts in her breeding career—two were kept stallions, Orcland John Darling and Orcland Don Darling—and one colt was gelded. Sadly, the chestnut mare died from a lightning strike when she was only 15 years old, the day before the aging Ulendon was put down. Anna Darling and Ulendon had many beautiful foals together, and they are buried near each other on a hill overlooking the former Orcland Farm.

At only 12, Orcland John Darling was diagnosed with an incurable, malignant tumor. His owners, Ruth and Lyman Orcutt, chose to give their Champion stallion a peaceful passing before the ravages of the cancer took hold. Orcland John Darling left our world never knowing the face of unbearable pain.

He is buried on that grassy hill in West Newbury, Massachussetts, and he rests in peace next to his brother, Orcland Don Darling—near their parents, Ulendon and Anna Darling.

Orcland John Darling sired an impressive foal crop during his yearlong stud duties for UConn, including the World Champion, UC Archer. Other standouts include UC Acrobat, UC Carillion and UC Hopeful. He made many friends and fans during his all-too-short time on this Earth.

Orcland John Darling, 2012

UVM Viking

UVM Flash-UVM Kathy
Born: 1970
University of Connecticut Herd Sire from 1978-1979

This spectacular two-year-old stallion….won great acclaim last year as a
yearling with his floating effortless trot with animation to burn.
~1972 Rapidan River Farm Advertisment, *The Morgan Horse*
Magazine.

An alluring chestnut grandson of the immortal Upwey Ben Don, UVM
Viking was a striking stallion with a large, tapered star on his forehead and
a white sock on his left hind fetlock. He was bred by Dr. Donald Balch, the
then-Director of the University of Vermont Morgan Horse Farm.

I had the distinct honor of speaking with Dr. Balch about UVM Viking. I
called him one evening, and as soon as I said "I would love to talk with you
about UVM Viking," I could immediately sense the deep admiration he had
for this horse. I let my open-ended question linger in the air and allowed Dr.
Balch to share his vivid memories of Viking, the phone cradled on my neck
and shoulder; my pen hurriedly jotting notes.

When UVM Viking came into the world in 1970, Dr. Balch was instantly
drawn to the handsome golden-red colt. As he matured, he displayed
floating gaits, flagging his tail like a stag as he trotted about. His nostrils took
in volumes of air, blowing and snorting with each stride. He possessed a
superstar quality from the get-go. Dr. Balch was possessive of his Morgan
horses like they were his children, thus, he made sure the outstanding ones
went to excellent homes where their talents would be properly showcased. As
a promising yearling, Dr. Balch's beloved UVM Viking was sold to Rapidan
River Farm in Lignum, Virginia where he became a foundation sire for the
farm's growing Morgan breeding program.

UVM Viking blossomed in Virginia, as Dr. Balch knew he would. When
UVM Viking was a mere two years old, he was crowned Eastern Grand
Champion Stallion, and thus began his successful show and breeding career.

Thanks to John and Marjorie Hagan of Rapidan River Farm, UVM Viking
was herd stallion at UConn for a full year—1978-1979.

His UConn-bred progeny include Sleipnir Farm's much–loved mare, the lovely UC Cinnamon, who floated at the trot and flagged her tail just like her sire. UVM Viking was also the sire of the popular UConn riding program mount, the chestnut gelding UC Danegeld. Other UConn-breds by UVM Viking also include UC Leprechaun, UC Peppermint, UC Stanza, UC First Edition and UC Valhalla.

UVM Viking was strong-headed, dauntless and athletic; a flashy mover with attitude and presence, with a shimmering golden coat. With his neck arched, showcasing his strength, UVM Viking kept handlers on toes and audiences in awe.

"Viking left quite an impression on you, didn't he?" I asked Dr. Balch. "I can picture Viking like I picture some people," he replied.

Dr. Balch paused briefly to reflect on the memories of his colt. Then, as he spoke, my pen captured the quietly profound words of Dr. Donald Balch:

I will never forget Viking.

UVM Viking, 2012

47

UC Ringmaster

Waseeka's Showtime-UC Lyric
Born: 1978
University of Connecticut Herd Sire from 1980-1982, 2001-2009

The Great Red Horse.
~Horse World Magazine

He completed my life.
~Owner Cheryl Orcutt

The year was 1977. Star Wars was the movie to see, Studio 54 was the place to be and gasoline was 63 cents a gallon.

Dr. Al Cowan, head of UConn's Animal Science department, and Professor Nathan Hale were on a quest for new blood for the University's Morgan herd. They wanted a stallion of regal bearing with spark and substance.

What they found was Waseeka's Showtime, bred and owned by John Lydon, trainer at Waseeka Farm of Charlton, Massachusetts. Waseeka's Showtime was called the "most beautiful Morgan horse that ever lived" and to those who saw the commanding bay stallion in the flesh, this was not an overstatement.

Waseeka's Showtime was a future World Champion stallion when Al Cowan and Nathan Hale met him. The stallion, with his upright, small ears, deep violet-brown eyes and thick, muscle-creased neck, was a wondrous vision. He possessed a glossy, dappled coat complete with a flash of white on his finely chiseled face. He moved with bold purpose and rippled with strength and beauty.

Waseeka's Showtime could not be denied; Cowan and Hale found their ideal stallion. In the hope that he would give a fine colt to the UConn herd, he was bred to UConn's two best mares, the jet-black UC Fascination and the bright bay UC Lyric.

The breeding did not take with UC Fascination, but it was a success with UC Lyric.

On June 30, 1978, the foal was born. There, in the straw, under the protective eye of UC Lyric, was a majestic-looking newborn colt, as red as a ruby, with a brilliant white star set perfectly between his eyes. As elegant as his dam and as grand as his sire, it was instantly apparent that this foal was The One.

Horse barn manager Bruce Walters couldn't get to the phone fast enough.

"You need to see this colt," Walters exclaimed to Dr. Cowan, his voice buzzing with excitement through the telephone wire.

He's the most beautiful foal I have ever seen.

The colt's eyes, reminiscent of his beautiful dam's, were large, soulful and frighteningly intelligent; and his pert ears were a carbon copy of his sire's. His legs were straight and strong, his face slightly dished, with wide-set eyes. His coat eventually dried to a deep cherry color with tones of dark amber. The foal was a gleaming jewel-toned Morgan with no visible flaw.

Al Cowan named the newborn "Ringmaster," as he was certain that this strong-boned crimson colt would dominate the show ring. The new blood, UConn's hope, had arrived.

UC Ringmaster was an animated colt that delighted the horse barn staff and visitors. One UConn student, Animal Science major Patti DeWet, had the honor of starting the precocious youngster's early training. Ringmaster proved himself to be a challenging horse to train; however, he was a highly intelligent creature with natural ability and immense talent. He lifted his legs high in a trot, possessed supreme balance and carriage and perked his ears so upright that they nearly touched at the tips. The charismatic colt demonstrated his superstar qualities early on and soon Patti and UC Ringmaster were winning ribbons at local shows. The future showed glimmering promise for UConn's son.

As a three-year-old, he caught the eye of prominent Morgan horse breeder and trainer, Lyman Orcutt, who had previously judged the horse and pinned a large blue and red rosette on his bridle. Orcutt didn't forget the garnet-red colt, and when UConn dispersed some of their herd, Al Cowan approached him about purchasing Ringmaster. Orcutt didn't need a lot of time to think about the prospect of having 'Ring' at his farm, as he and his wife, Cheryl, were besotted with the gifted young star. Especially Cheryl, who deemed him 'adorable.'

The Orcutts happily purchased UC Ringmaster, and brought him home to their Juniper Hill Farm in Peterborough, New Hampshire.

The Orcutts continued Ring's education; Lyman drove the young horse and Cheryl rode him. Cheryl soon discovered that Ring had a butter-soft mouth and could be ridden primarily with leg and weight aids. He learned to pick his head up and look around him, but he still managed to stay in the bridle in complete contact with his rider. He was a thrilling ride.

Around the barn, Ringmaster was highly perceptive to mood and tone of voice; he loved to be touched and groomed, treasuring the time spent with his humans.

Ring had a pleasing and friendly personality, too. He would talk and nicker and snuffle frequently, even when he was alone in his stall. He adored attention and seemed to request it from everyone who came within earshot, but his favorite person was clearly Cheryl Orcutt. He was fond of resting his head on Cheryl's shoulder, gently blowing in her ear. He also enjoyed putting his lips to Cheryl's cheek and talking softly to her. She never feared that he would be mean or dangerous and their bond deepened because of their unwavering mutual trust. She was convinced that this stallion was unlike any horse she had ever encountered.

"He was a person," Cheryl would say of him many years later. "He was never just a horse."

A young UC Ringmaster, *circa* 1981

His road to superstardom also led him to Newtown, Connecticut and the farm of Richard and Andrea Haas. Here, he stood at stud and began training with the farm manager, Leslie "Les" Parker.

One memorable day, Cheryl Orcutt visited her red stallion at the busy farm. She requested that Les long-line Ringmaster. After what Cheryl described as a "clatter and bang," due to Les getting the horse to focus on the task at hand, Les and Ringmaster turned a corner and trotted up a straightaway and it was as if storm clouds had parted. Cheryl saw what she had been looking for: a partnership of man and horse that promised greatness. It was kismet.

Cheryl had seen the horse she always knew was there. He carried his head with confidence, engaged his hindquarters under his body and kept his small ears forward and alert the whole time. It was as if Ring was saying, "So this is what I am supposed to do!" He was suddenly a new horse.

Cheryl's heart was pounding as she approached Les and Ring after their awe-inspiring impromptu performance. She contained her excitement in front of Les, a soft-spoken and skilled horseman she had known since she was a kid.

"So," Cheryl asked Les as nonchalantly as possible. "Would you be interested in working this horse?"

"I thought you were just going to breed him," Les replied.

"Well, I'm thinking maybe we can work him. Interested?"

"Let's shoe him up and we'll see."

This quick-spoken agreement marked the beginning of the legendary partnership between the charismatic Morgan stallion and his trainer—and what a partnership it was. Les would wrap his long legs around Ringmaster's barrel and gently squeeze his sides and Ring would respond by bowing his neck, flaring his nostrils and moving effortlessly into his gaits. The reins were slack and the bit would barely rub the corners of his soft mouth, but Ring would do exactly what was asked of him, every time, and it seemed that he and Les were made for each other. Even in the show ring, the young stallion did not distract easily and he was as dependable as the sunset: young horses can sometimes get too excited in a canter and will run off with their riders fighting for balance in the saddle. In order to gain better control, a rider could ask their horse for a canter in a corner instead of on the long side of the arena. Such measures were not needed with the superstar-in-the-making, however. UC Ringmaster was so well broke, so brilliantly trained, that he could canter anywhere in the show ring and always come back to his rider. He presented such a confident and beautiful picture that many in the audience were speechless with mouths agape as they watched him work. He was suddenly *the* horse to beat. He possessed a fluid and perfect road trot and much to the amazement of judges and spectators, he stayed balanced and on his feet as he extended his gait to eat up the ground. He also had a slow, controlled canter that was a textbook perfect three-beat rocking horse gait, and it made him a serious contender as an equitation horse.

And he was *red!* The burnished auburn stallion demanded attention every time his black polished hooves hit the russet sand in the arena. As he entered his classes, time seemed to stop as his big, white-rimmed eyes connected with every spectator in the stands. Al Cowan had chosen the name of his horse wisely.

Regional wins in Connecticut, Massachusetts and New York paved the way to his first World Championship competition in Oklahoma in 1991 when Ring was a 13-year-old. When the stallion strutted into the arena, the crowds clapped and hooted, the applause echoing off of the structure.

He would spot a judge in the corner of his eye, open his blazing nostrils wide and give a self-assured snort like he was a bellows feeding a fire. He would fill his heart and lungs and grow before the crowd. *Look at me,* he seemed to say, *you know you want to pin one of those big ribbons on my bridle!* Sometimes, the show judges would ask for a workout from Ring just for the sheer pleasure of watching him doing what he loved best.

Sure enough, UC Ringmaster was crowned World Champion English Pleasure horse.

When most horses would win World Championship titles at seven or eight, it was highly unusual for a horse approaching middle age to compete, let alone win, at such a level. But Ring was no ordinary horse; he was a son of the cavalry: brave, strong and unflappable. He had no soundness, health or training issues. He was, as Horse World magazine called him, *The Great Red Horse.*

When Ring returned home from his World Championship win, he was given a year off from the rigors of competition. Cheryl kept his mind and body in optimal condition, jogging him on a moss-covered knoll with a slight incline. The moss helped keep the spring in his trot and the incline ensured that his muscles stayed show-ready fit. The World Champion was entered in the Grand Nationals, giving them one month to get Ringmaster ready. In 1993, he was off to Oklahoma City for another World Championship competition—he automatically qualified because of his 1991 win. Could Ring do it again, at 15 years of age, competing with younger horses that had been actively showing all season? Would the trip to Oklahoma City unnerve him, shake his confidence?

Some horses get worked up and nervous when they travel and can go off their feed and water, but Ringmaster was unaffected. He ate with his usual gusto, drank gallons of water and kept his naptime at 3pm everyday. He nickered and whuffled in his stall as he chowed down on his hay. Another World Championship? *No worries!*

Because Ring hadn't shown all season, he was dismissed by some as being too old and too unfit to win the title again. But, when the English Pleasure class was announced, throngs of people on foot and in golf carts headed for the show ring to see The Great Red Horse perform. Some were running to get the best seat—suddenly the English Pleasure class was *the* show to see.

It was nearly standing room only when the class started. When Ring entered the arena, he thrilled the crowd, holding them in rapt attention. There he was.

With his body bristling with muscle, UC Ringmaster carried Les Parker around the show ring like the Master he was. Every step was artistically and technically perfect; horse and rider were one entity on that day.

When it came time to declare the winner of the class, announcer Bill Carrington asked the crowd to call out the winning number and the arena filled up with the deafening roar of Ring's number yelled out in unison. The other competitors tipped their hats to the 15-year-old stallion and his long-legged rider as they made their victory pass around the arena. As Les and Ring trotted towards the exit gate, Les held the slack reins in his teeth and held his arms out sideways. UC Ringmaster never missed a beat.

The crowd went wild, erupting in applause.

One judge was moved to exclaim that Ringmaster was "too brilliant to be a Pleasure horse."

As he performed his famous extended and balanced road trot, another judge proclaimed as Ring's legs stretched over the earth and found his fourth gear, "he can't be doing that!"

But he *was* doing that. Every once in a while, a truly incredible horse comes along that makes people question the supernatural equine brilliance set in motion before their eyes. UC Ringmaster was that horse.

After he won the 1993 World Championship, a woman and her two little girls visited the show barns and asked if they could meet the famous Ringmaster. The stallion particularly loved children and was careful and kind when they were in his company.

Les took the woman and the two golden-haired girls, who were no more than five or six years old, to see the Champion. Les opened the stall door and Ring walked over to the children and bent his head down to greet them. He softly blew his warm breath into one girl's blonde tresses and rested his gray velvet muzzle against her cheek. The girl visibly shivered.

"You can touch him," Cheryl said to the girl, encouraging in her what would most likely be a lifelong love of horses.

As the girl reached over and stroked the gentle stallion's nose, she was transformed. In a hushed, wonder-filled voice, the girl said:

We call him the fire-breathing dragon...

UC Ringmaster set a new standard for the Morgan English Pleasure horse and he was touted as the English Pleasure horse of the century. He proved that the impossible could be done, that a horse could stay perfectly in balance as he propelled his legs forward in an extension, and that a horse can keep his ears upright the entire time simply because he was joyful. He could be a child's pocket pony, but as soon as the bridle was slipped over his head, it was game on. Cheryl recalls when a competitor saw Ring in the warm up area before a show, he saluted the magnificent red stallion with a wave of his hand and said to Les Parker, "this one is yours."

In the business of breeding, Ring was a complete gentleman who had a bit of a thing for black mares. He would trumpet to a lovely raven gal and proclaim that she was his, even if she never looked up. He could tell if a mare was in season almost immediately.

His gallant and enthusiastic breeding skills produced many successful progeny, including UC Top Brass, World Champion Gelding; UC Merlin, World Champion Working Hunter; UC Serendipity, Reserve World Champion Working Hunter; UC Rianna, multiple USEF National Horse of the Year Morgan Carriage Champion; UC Town Crier, World Champion Equitation Mount; and UC Tee Rose, Low Hunter Champion, amongst many others. He also sired UConn's first embryo-transfer horse, UC Wilde Mark. His son, UC Top Hat, was a show-stopping Road Hack Champion that has the great honor of a namesake Connecticut Morgan Horse Show trophy.

In March 2001, Juniper Hill Farm's operation was winding down and Cheryl made the selfless decision to part with her best friend and send him back to the University of Connecticut's beautiful Storrs campus to enjoy his retirement from competition.

Many wondered why Cheryl let go of her beloved red stallion, as he meant so much to her and to Lyman. But, that is precisely why she let him go: her love for the Morgan stallion was so strong that she put her own personal feelings and agenda aside and solely considered her horse's happiness. Juniper Hill Farm was no longer the bustling horse operation it once was; many of the horses were sold and the farm took on an air of quiet and graceful splendor. Ring was lonely. For the first time, Cheryl saw the slightest hint of depression in the stallion's eyes, and it broke her heart. He needed to be in the center of all of the attention again—he needed to whinny at the black mares and nicker at the co-eds as they mucked his stall. Ring knew how to speak to Cheryl and he was quite clear in his request of his favorite human:

I want to be part of a big horse family again. I love you but that is where I belong.

Cheryl listened and honored her great horse's wishes. Back at his birthplace at UConn, he was given a large, airy corner stall where many admirers could see him and stroke his muzzle. He could talk to barn visitors all day long and tell them his stories of ribbons and trophies. He would tell them all about the quiet man with the long legs who rode him to victory and the nice lady who let him kiss her cheek. And he could brag about his many talented children. He could be around his horse friends all day, every day.

Still fertile at his advancing age, he could make even more sons and daughters that would win ribbons of their own and delight the hearts of their owners. In June 2010, at 32 years of age, the gentle graying stallion was loaded onto a trailer headed for the Big E Fairgrounds in West Springfield, Massachusetts.

Accompanied by his human friends from UConn, he was on his way to his induction into the Connecticut Morgan Horse Association Hall of Fame.

The arena awaited him, yet again. It called to him, sparking glorious memories of victories past. The crowd was there to see the one and only UC Ringmaster.

As UConn horse barn manager John Bennett drove UC Ringmaster through the theatrical fog machine mist to *Stayin' Alive* by the Bee Gees, the crowd roared once again for the Great Red Horse. He trotted out, confident and full of spirit, his famous little ears pointing skyward the entire time. He was a marvel, a 32-year-old stallion that was not only as completely sound, but also as completely thrilling, as he was in his youth. He drank in the applause, a familiar and comforting sound that he had not heard for many years. He was a Champion again, performing for his devoted fans—it was a feeling he knew well and it gladdened his strong UConn Morgan heart.

As *We Are The Champions* by Queen was played over the arena sound system, Ringmaster did one last victory walk in front of his adoring crowd.

He was as quiet and as still as a statue in the middle of the Big E Fairgrounds arena as he waited for his Hall of Fame rosette to be hung around his neck. Cheryl Orcutt walked over to her old friend and he recognized her immediately. UC Ringmaster leaned into Cheryl, as he always did when he was near her, and she put one reassuring arm over his withers and patted his shoulder.

My friend.

As The Connecticut Morgan Horse Association Hall of Fame welcomed UC Ringmaster into its esteemed ranks, his fans cheered one more time for the twice-over World Champion.

Today, UC Ringmaster, the grand statesman, leads an unhurried, but active, life at the University of Connecticut. Gray hairs have sprouted on his face, and his eyes are inquisitive and alert. His back has the sway and dip of an elderly horse, but he has not lost that look of a two-time World Champion, his flawless conformation and handsome head are still apparent. He is a dazzling equine.

Still a lover of human company, Ring enjoys his grooming sessions immensely. His eyes close and his whiskered upper lip trembles as the rubber curry comb scratches the itchy spot by his withers. Relaxed, his head dips low as the layer of dead hair is brushed away to reveal his famous auburn coat.

The kind, old horse, always a gentleman, provides us with an illustrious reminder of the true character and allure of the University of Connecticut Morgan horse.

UC Ringmaster has made UConn proud.

Addendum
UC Ringmaster
June 30, 1978-November 20, 2012.

On November 20, 2012, the two-time World Champion, UC Ringmaster, was put to rest due to declining health. He was 34.

It was clear and sunny—mild, with a twinge of apple-scented crispness lingering in the late autumn air. It was a lovely day created just for a Champion.

I had visited Ring on November 17, and could see he was not himself. But, ever the gracious host, he perked his ears forward and allowed me to gently scratch his hindquarters through the stall bars. His muzzle quivered a little as my fingernails combed his famous red coat.

His strong cavalry heart was beating slower, and the joy of being alive was diminishing for the old stallion. I savored every moment with my friend, as it could be the last time I could ever visit with him. Time can be so fleeting, and life, with its passing, can remind us that an extra moment may not happen.

I returned the next day to see if he was still with us. To my delight, when I peered in his stall, he was enjoying some hay, a little perkier than the day before. He lifted his head for a few seconds to politely regard me, and he offered a barely audible nicker. The nicker was so soft, so unlike the robust, animated snufflings of his younger days, it seemed to take such effort for him to produce the sounds. But, still the gentleman, he wanted to thank me for visiting. It was such a sweet gesture that I felt myself catching my breath. I snapped his picture at that moment. He posed like he always did; ears up and eyes wide. Always The Great Red Horse.

And, with that weak whuffle, he said goodbye to me. I told him I loved him and that goodbye only means "see you later." I promised that I would write a beautiful book for him, and generations will remember him and his many children and grandchildren. He lowered his head to lip some hay, and wanting to give him some peace to enjoy his meal, I walked away from his stall, my heart heavy as lead. I felt a well of sadness start to simmer inside of me, so I made my way down the barn aisle and around the corner, and exited the barn. The outside greeted me with brisk air and sunshine, but I could not stop the tears from escaping and rolling down my face. The cold November morning chilled them on my cheeks.

I knew I would never see UC Ringmaster again. When the sun set that day, illuminating the sky with fiery reds and pinks, I envisioned the magical stallion conquering the world, not once, but twice. He was there, in those brilliant clouds, lifting his legs high as he danced across the early evening sky.

I will think of him every time I see a beautiful red sunset.

UC Ringmaster, 2006

A Wish for an Old Friend

I wish you sunbeams in your mane
I wish you wind under your hooves

I wish on a sparkling star tonight
for wishes that come true.

~Helen Scanlon, 11/17/2012
for UC Ringmaster

Chantwood Command

Waseeka's In Command-Ru Lee's Fair Lass
Born: 1977
University of Connecticut Herd Sire from 1986-1987

He was a cute powerhouse.
~Kathy Pelletier, UConn Assistant Barn Manager

Chantwood Command was leased to UConn for the 1986-1987 season and was used mostly for student projects and for frozen semen research. A handsome little bay, he was a flashy showman. In 1981, he won both the Indy 500 Jr. Park Saddle Championship and the Gold Cup Reserve Jr. Park Saddle Stallion.

In addition to his superstar presence, he had a willing attitude and wonderful ground manners. He was one of the first stallions that Kathy Pelletier handled, and she remembers him as a polite horse that was not pushy in the least.

Chantwood Command had an impressive pedigree that featured such standouts as his sire, Waseeka's In Command, his grandsire, Waseeka's Nocturne and multiple Champion and highly successful sire, Upwey Ben Don. He sired a few foals for UConn, including UC Desiree and UC Justa Flirt.

After his brief stint at UConn, records state he was sold through the Fantasia Farm dispersal sale, and he continued his breeding career.

Even though his time at UConn was short, memories of this polite stallion can bring smiles to those who knew him.

Chantwood Command, 2012

UC Doc Daniels
UVM Elite-UC Topaz
Born: 1987
University of Connecticut Herd Sire from 1990-2010

He was the Charismatic Ambassador. ~Kathy Pelletier

He would walk through fire if you asked him. ~Mary O'Donovan

Veterinarian and UConn alumna Mary O'Donovan acquired the horse of her dreams, UC Doc Daniels, in August of 2010. She never thought it would happen. Every time she asked John Bennett if she could have him, his response was, "Mary, he's staying here until he breathes his last."

However, when the stallion, now nearing his mid-twenties, sported an abnormally swollen testicle and a drop in his fertility, everything changed.

The grim diagnosis was testicular cancer, and Doc would require risky castration surgery in order to stop the cancer from spreading. Fate stepped in and Mary not only offered the pensioned stallion a home, but she offered to perform the life-saving procedure herself.

Mary now had her dream horse, the Morgan gentleman known as UC Doc Daniels.

Doc's story started in 1987 when the stallion UVM Elite was bred to the lovely mare, UC Topaz. The result was an achingly gorgeous bay colt with a large searching eye and a bright, uniquely shaped star in the middle of his forehead. He was named after Dr. Willard Daniels, the much-respected Animal Science professor and large animal veterinarian who helped deliver the colt. Dr. Daniels announced his retirement shortly after the colt's birth.

UC Doc Daniels was a tall, leggy youngster that could prove to be a handling challenge. He was playful and curious, and he was as smart as a raven. When he matured and learned what was expected of him, he became easier to handle.

61

His limitless youthful exuberance burned away to reveal a breath-catching stallion with a personality befitting a charming aristocrat. His bay coat was a rich red-brown that reflected a prism of sunlight in each strand of hair, and his mane and tail cascaded like tumbling black waves.

Doc possessed a correct old-style Morgan look with wide-set, intelligent eyes, straight, strong legs and a powerful neck. He was a classic Morgan, hence, he was a natural for the UConn breeding program.

UC Doc Daniels gives Santa and UConn President Harry Hartley a ride; John Bennett, Jr. at the reins, 1992

As a flashy two-year-old, he readily won his classes with students showing him. The stallion proved himself reliable and gentle, and he could be entrusted with the not-so-experienced handlers. He taught many students the finer points of in-hand showing and carriage driving, in addition to siring many impressive foals.

In the breeding shed, Doc was attentive, gentle and a bit of an equine Romeo. Mary recalls how Doc would always approach a mare at her head first, nuzzling and nickering at her the entire time. Some stallions could be somewhat aggressive and "all business," but not Doc Daniels—he was always respectful and romantic with his ladies-in-waiting.

UC Doc Daniels possessed a special kind of dazzle that was befitting of a royal or a rock star. When it was show time, it was all about Doc Daniels. He was full of himself but not boastful. He demanded attention, but would thank you for noticing. He was proud, but never vain. He was, as Kathy Pelletier says, "a charismatic ambassador for the University of Connecticut."

He would cart Governors, University Presidents and even Santa Claus in parades and events. Each passenger in his carriage was given his fluid, floating trot, high neck carriage and unmistakable Morgan air of nobility. He would keep a cool head in every situation—even in a parade through the streets of Hartford, the sound of his hooves echoing off the tall buildings in a near-deafening din of clip-clops. With his ears straight up and his eye whites blazing, he would beam his easy pride to the adoring crowd.

He knew they were all there to see him—the one and only Doc Daniels, the brilliant bay stallion from the hills of UConn.

Now, fully recovered from his surgery, UC Doc Daniels enjoys rolling in a muddy paddock and spending time with Mary, the woman who proclaimed him the "the most beautiful horse at the UConn barn."

Mary's voice fills with a smile as she speaks of her beloved horse and how as a student, she fumbled with a complicated carriage harness and Doc Daniels just stood there patiently waiting for her to figure it out. He stood square and calm, careful not to get the seemingly miles-long leather reins under his hooves and around his legs. He would even lower his head to help Mary put on his breast collar. Mary has not forgotten his many kindnesses to her and she has given him an easy retirement, making his comfort a top priority. UC Doc Daniels is fit and happy.

UC Doc Daniels is a treasured friend and a wise teacher, still a proud ambassador of the University of Connecticut Morgan, and of the Morgan breed itself.

UC Doc Daniels, *circa* 1992

UC Show Biz

Waseeka's Showtime-UC Lyric
Born: 1988
University of Connecticut Herd Sire from 1992-1996

I trusted him with everybody; he was so gentle. He was the best.
~Lloyd Crawford

An alert, spirited bay full brother to two-time World Champion UC Ringmaster, UC Show Biz was born in 1988 and was used in the UConn breeding program starting in 1992. It was hoped that the genetic gods could produce magic once again with the pairing of the great stallion Waseeka's Showtime and the lovely mare UC Lyric. Although Show Biz was not a replica of his older brother, UC Ringmaster, he did respectably in his show career and he sired some nice foals.

Show Biz was also different from Ringmaster in personality. Where Ringmaster was a horse that could be in-your-face social and chatty, Show Biz would be with people in his own time and on his own terms. He was, according to Kathy Pelletier, "a bit of a stinker" when he was young. Show Biz had energy—lots of it—and he could, at times, "climb the walls," according to John Bennett. His fiery personality meant that most students were not allowed to handle him. He was a horse that required expert, firm leadership, and he was a supreme teacher in this respect—one must never be complacent around a powerful and headstrong stallion.

His get include UC Fancy Bizness, UC Biz E Flirting, UC Show Girl and UC Spring Break. His son, UC Arthur L., "Artie," was a wonderful, versatile drill team horse that loved to eat Sweet Tarts candy. Artie was a favorite mount for many UConn and community lesson students.

UC Show Biz was the kind of stallion that would garner whispers when he displayed his power, his black mane and tail whipping around with each leap and stride. He had beautiful, dark eyes and a gorgeous head—every inch a Morgan.

In 2000, Show Biz was sold to trainer Lloyd Crawford and Dr. David Rossi. Crawford, a veteran trainer who trained students to many World Championships, bought the stallion to teach Rossi how to ride. And what a teacher he was. Because of Rossi's time astride Show Biz, he won Amateur

64

of the Year with the horse EB Brass Ring.

Show Biz, now a gelding, taught many students, mostly junior competitors. He was such a patient and effective teacher that his young charges went on to be World Champions in their first year out. Show Biz, according to Crawford, "made everyone feel special."

Lloyd Crawford proudly stated that UC Show Biz was the best horse he ever owned.

> *He was gentle as a kitten and would endure anything—floppy legs, poor balance. I never had a problem with that horse, ever.*

David Rossi and his horse developed a tight bond during their time together. Rossi, an emergency room doctor, would often work 12-hour shifts—but he would always want to ride his horse the moment he arrived home. Tension from the day's crises would dissolve as soon as Rossi was in the saddle. Show Biz would trot out, ears perked, eyes wide.

Suddenly, with the familiar squeak of saddle leather, all was right in the world.

UC Show Biz: the animated colt, the confident stallion, and the wise teacher. He was always a horse that simply gave his all.

UC Show Biz, *circa* 1992

UC Toronado

Tedwin Taurean-UC Fascination
Born: 1990
University of Connecticut Herd Sire from 1994-2001

> *My favorite thing about him is that he's beautiful and so perfect in every way.*
> ~Jade Lussier, age 16.

UC Toronado is a gleaming ebony son of multi-titled World Champion and Hall-of-Famer, Tedwin Taurean, and the UConn-bred black mare UC Fascination.

I first glimpsed UC Toronado during one of my walks around the UConn barns in the late 90's.

As I walked by the stalls talking to the mares and polo ponies, I stopped short at a stall that housed a magnificent black stallion with a thick mane and a high, muscled crest. The name card on the stall read "UC Toronado."

"Oh my, who do we have here?" I whispered to myself. He had a dished face and a tapered muzzle with large, air-gulping nostrils. His wavy foretop fringed his brilliant, large eyes. He was, simply and purely, beautiful.

The black horse was curious about me and I spoke softly to him. He was receptive, flicking his ears in time to my voice.

The equine that stood before me was dazzling and unapologetically grand. His coat resembled polished obsidian and his mane fell in glossy ribbons about his neck and withers. He regarded me cautiously, and I could feel his warm breath on my skin.

UC Toronado, although officially listed in the American Morgan Horse Registry as a "brown," was black as ink. He smoldered and twitched with muscle. He radiated power. His eyes were volcanoes, erupting with red-hot embers. He demanded respect.

He was the Black Stallion of UConn.

Many UConn alumni have stories about the mighty "Tor." The imposing stallion was not for the inexperienced; he had no qualms about testing his

UC Toronado, *circa* 1994

limits with the human at the end of the lead shank. But, even the experienced
could be taken by surprise. One alumna recalls the day she was cleaning
his stall, and turned her back on Tor for a whisper of second—and in that
moment, Toronado grabbed her by the back of her t-shirt with his teeth and
tossed her out of his stall, unhurt, but shaken. He had managed to grab the
cloth of the shirt and not her flesh, but he got his point across.

"Never made that mistake again," the alumna told me.

John Bennett recalls Tor as a strong colt that could "go off his feet" and be
challenging to handle. However, his energy and spirit served him well—Tor
had a successful show career, winning Grand Champion stallion in Pleasure
Driving at Maine Morgan. He was a strong and elegant mover, proving that
he was a formidable presence in and out of the show ring.

Kathy Pelletier admired Tor a great deal. She said he was never mean, but
was misunderstood at times. If you were clear and confident with him, you
had no problems. Tor would respect anyone who was a fearless leader. He
was a valiant sort, but could have a sense of fun and Kathy recalls his frisky
and playful demeanor with a smile.

UC Toronado had the ancient procreation instinct firmly ingrained in his
DNA, and Janice Callahan, Coach of the UConn Equestrian Team, recalls
how he always "had breeding on his mind." He passed on his bold character

and stunning good looks to his foals, and many of them were stars in the show arena and on the Drill Team. Some of his outstanding UConn progeny include UC Hope and Courage, UC Tee Time, UC Leonardo, UC Cadberry, UC Braveheart, UC Courage Under Fire and UC Moonshadow.

As a teacher and a driving and riding horse, he could freely offer unforgettable moments to his students. In 2000, Courtnay (Henninger) Lawrence's Independent Study at UConn introduced her to the magic that is UC Toronado—she had never ridden a stallion before she got on his back. Courtnay's passion was saddleseat, and she recalls the day she rode Tor after another student had admitted defeat with him:

> *When I climbed aboard it was a great feeling. He was soft in the full bridle, supple under my legs, and responsive to my seat. We nailed both our leads and Mr. Bennett praised our ride.*

As a driving horse, Courtnay found him to be steady and consistent in the lines—and he moved with the confident, forward energy of a seasoned and successful show Morgan. Courtnay admired UC Toronado and the times spent with him are still clear in her mind.

In 2001, he was sold to Daniel King and was used as a breeding stallion and work horse in the heart of Amish country in Lancaster, Pennsylvania. In 2004, he moved back to the Northeast, settling in Massachusetts. He was gelded that year, and at some point his name was changed to "Gideon."

Around 2009, he was introduced to a young girl by the name of Jade Lussier. She met him at her barn; he belonged to her friend who also rode. She saw him and immediately felt a connection. He was the most beautiful horse she had ever seen.

She recalls the time they first met:

> *He went to the back of his stall with his ears pinned back, but he let me put his halter on and walk him out and brush him. After that first time he was fine. He would look forward to me coming to get him. His ears would go up when he saw me.*

It seems the connection was reciprocated. UC Toronado, now affectionately known as "Giddy," took center stage in the heart of a girl who had always dreamed of riding a proud, black steed. And ride they did. Jade won Giddy's trust and although he would stand stock still and refuse to move for other riders, he trotted out with his floating, Champion grace when Jade was astride him. They were awarded ribbons and accolades at horse shows in Woodstock, Connecticut and the Tri-State horse shows.

In the horse show world, some UConn alumni thought they had spotted the elusive Black Stallion of UConn—and was he carrying a young girl on his back, winning the rosettes? Yes, he was. The big, tough stallion was a sweetheart underneath it all. One is reminded of the classic quote: *Every horse deserves, at least once, to be loved by a little girl.*

Today, he enjoys time in his paddock, rolling in the dirt and visiting with his best friend, a Morgan horse named Nickie. But, if you gaze into those dark, flashing eyes, you can still see the kingly Black Stallion of UConn.

Calling To The Mares, 2012

UC Domination
UC Doc Daniels-UC Aria
Born: 2004
Junior Herd Sire

He is a blast to ride and he loves to snort and show off when he has an audience. ~Caitlin Lewis

UC Domination, a son of the beloved UC Doc Daniels and UC Aria, is a handsome bay with a quick mind, a happy personality and a trustworthy nature. UConn student Caitlin Lewis first met him during the winter break of 2007-2008, after learning to drive with "Dom's" sire, UC Doc Daniels, that fall.

Dom caught Caitlin's attention with his striking good looks and his endearing goofiness whenever someone tried to muck out his stall; she was compelled to ask John Bennett if she could work with him. Bennett could see how much Caitlin admired the young stallion, so he agreed and UC Domination became Caitlin's Independent Study project.

Caitlin learned much from Bennett's patient instruction—together, they long lined, drove and started Dom under saddle. Dom was a quick study, and soon Caitlin found herself showing the little bay at the 2008 Connecticut Morgan Horse Show. Dom didn't win any ribbons that day, but he was so well-behaved that his promise was undeniable.

The following summer when Dom was five years old, they won their first blue ribbon in a Classic Pleasure Saddle class at the Massachusetts Morgan Horse Show. If Caitlin was nervous, Dom proved his trustworthiness and "never put a foot wrong." Their bond was easily displayed by a thrilling partnership in the show ring.

Many other show successes followed. In 2011, UC Domination, shown by Caitlin Lewis, has won: Champion, Road Hack at the Connecticut Morgan Horse Show; English Pleasure Amateur Class, Connecticut Summer Classic;

and Reserve Champion, Road Hack, Vermont Spring Classic.

Dom has also shown great early success as a junior stallion—his filly, UC Mischief Managed, won the Filly Foal Class at the 2011 New England Morgan Show.

UC Domination possesses a gentle, unflappable personality like his sire, yet he knows when there's a camera around and is notorious for strutting and posing when he hears the shutter click. He enjoys being lavished with loving attention, and can be a playful rabble-rouser with a mind of his own. Caitlin says Dom is a pleasant, agreeable soul that has "never pinned his ears back at another horse or person."

UC Domination is a shining young star at the University of Connecticut, and many more Championships and successful offspring are in his future.

UC Doc Sanchez

UC Doc Daniels-UC Tee Time
Born: 2007
Junior Herd Sire

> *....I was so proud of that horse for trying so hard for me that I couldn't hold back my emotions. The rest of the class was literally a blur, I could barely see through my tears. I have ridden probably over 100 horses in my short life and I can confidently say I have NEVER felt that way on a horse before. We were literally one in that show ring; if I thought something he did it.* ~Kayleigh Meyer on winning a Championship on UC Doc Sanchez at Connecticut Morgan Horse Show

A delightful bay with a star just like his sire, UC Doc Sanchez is a hotshot in the show ring, dazzling audiences and wowing judges with his forward, high-headed, totally-in-the-bridle presence.

UC Doc Sanchez, named after the vet, Dr. Alfredo Sanchez, was a firecracker as a youngster, stepping high and weaving on and off the rail, too animated to even think about going in a straight line. Kayleigh Meyer, a freshman at the time, spotted the colt and knew she had to find a way to ride him—his energy was that of a Champion. She mustered up the courage to ask John Bennett if he would consider letting her assist with his training.

"Mr. Bennett, if he's not broke yet, I would love to be the one to do it," she asked.

"Well, Miss Kayleigh Meyer, this is University of Connecticut, the land of opportunity. Ask and you shall receive," was John Bennett's reply.

Kayleigh now had the honor of working with the captivating bay colt, and it was then that she fell in love with the Morgan breed.

John Bennett worked with Kayleigh, teaching her long lining and carriage driving with the seasoned professionals, UC Ringmaster and UC Doc Daniels. Kayleigh's confidence and skills grew and UC Doc Sanchez became her regular equine training project and partner. She taught the little stallion how to give "kisses" and cuddled with him as he napped in his stall. The two forged a strong bond that could be readily seen in the arena: under saddle, the bay was transformed into the "little stallion that could." He poured his soul into his work, with ears pricked and eyes wide, completely tuned into Kayleigh's cues.

Their teamwork was stunning to watch in action.

Their trust was translated into numerous Champion neck ribbons and the UConn Husky cheer from the grandstands.

UC Doc Sanchez, shown by Kayleigh Meyer, has already won the following accolades in his young and promising career:

> 2011: Reserve Champion Classic Pleasure Saddle, Connecticut Morgan Horse Show; Classic Pleasure Driving Champion and Classic Pleasure Saddle Reserve Champion, Connecticut Summer Classic Morgan Horse Show; Winner of the highly contested Classic Pleasure Junior horse class, Massachusetts Morgan Horse Show.

> 2012: Champion Classic Pleasure Saddle, Connecticut Morgan Horse Show

UC Doc Sanchez, with his charisma, sweet disposition, classic Morgan handsomeness and breathtaking flash is sure to make some beautiful Champion babies of his own. Keep your eye on this one!

UC Mastermind

UC Ringmaster-UC Faith
Born: 2009
Junior Herd Sire

UC Mastermind is an impressive golden chestnut that has the distinct privilege of carrying on the UC Ringmaster line.

Full of spark and spirit, he is sure to add some rosettes to the UConn trophy case.

This writer and fans of the acclaimed UC Ringmaster will be watching Mastermind's career with great interest.

Part Three
Heart and Spirit: The Mares

VC Sonata
HS '12

I Know the Way Home

Take the big step
The one that terrifies you
Yet thrills you at the same time
I will take care of you
For I know the way home.
            ~The Morgan Horse

Sheba

Osage-Nubia
Born: 1948
University of Connecticut Top-Producing Broodmare from 1951-1967
Foals Produced: 14

The beloved Matriarch.

Sheba was an amiable, blaze-faced chestnut mare that was brought to UConn, along with Mentor and three other mares, in 1951. She was one of two Government-bred mares that formed a strong, top-producing broodmare foundation for UConn. Sheba had straight, sound legs and granite-hard feet. She also possessed excellent conformation and was enchanting in her shimmering, sun-kissed coat.

Sheba was called "a veritable queen" and she produced fourteen foals in total. She was Reserve Champion Mare at the Eastern States Exposition in 1956, and she won the Mare and Foal class at the same show in 1959. She also placed second in the Mare and Foal class at the 1962 National Morgan Horse show. Sheba was consistently bred to the herd stallion, the National Champion, Panfield. Sheba and Panfield produced six full sisters, and as Dr. Al Cowan said, "their names are legend in UConn Morgan history." They were UC Serenade, UC Rhapsody, UC Melodie, UC Harmony and UC Reverie. Four of these Panfield-Sheba sisters remained at UConn, and some of the best horses in the UConn herd could be traced directly to UC Melodie and UC Rhapsody.

In 1966, Sheba produced the bay filly UC Heather by UConn herd stallion, Windcrest Don Again. She was an outstanding filly in type and quality, and as a two-year-old she was sold to Intrepid Farm in California. She was shown extensively on the West coast, and she went on to win an amazing 12 Grand Championships and two Reserves.

1968 was a heartbreaking year for the UConn Morgan horse program as the beloved Sheba was starting to show the effects of her advancing age. On

76

her last day, she could barely move about and she was humanely put to sleep when it was apparent she was suffering. She was 19.

Sadly, Sheba's last foal, UC Finale, died of a "tragic, unavoidable accident" that same year. Hearts were heavy with loss.

Working with horses can be a sad business. They are large, yet delicate, beasts that bond with us and allow us to sit upon their backs—the ultimate display of trust for a prey animal. We rejoice in their victories, we help them deliver their foals, we sleep next to them on a hay bale when they are sickly—praying to the equine gods for their recovery and health. Time does not matter; we follow the rhythm of their ancient clocks. Horses live in the now. They remind us to do the same. We cry when they leave us. Even when it is clearly their time, we are never quite ready to let them go. We want just one more ride. We want just one more grooming session, hands tracing the outline of bone and muscle—black muzzles searching pockets for hidden cookies. We want one more visit in the sun, the scent of wildflowers heavy in the air.

We want just one more shared moment.

Many felt that way about the wonderful mare named Sheba.

Sheba's beauty, grace and flawlessness are apparent in her descendants. Her star shone brightly.

Sheba, 1967

Sentana

Flyhawk-Sentola
Born: 1945
University of Connecticut Top-Producing Broodmare from 1954-1964
Foals Produced: 8

It is hoped that this mare, through her offspring, will be the foundation of one of the good future families in the Morgan breed. ~1952 Morgan Horse Magazine

Sentana, a beautiful, flaxen-maned chestnut mare, came to UConn in 1953, donated to the school by Mr. J. Harry Wood of Petersham, Massachusetts and St. Louis, Missouri.

Her sire was the mighty and versatile Flyhawk. Bred by Joseph C. Brunk, Flyhawk was a highly influential Morgan stallion with a stellar show and breeding career. The alert, bright-eyed stallion—that curiously loved to swim in deep water—won his last show in Western tack when he was loaned to a 7-year-old girl as a last-minute steed replacement at a Morgan event. He lived to age 32, and he retained his appealing disposition until his final day.

Sentana's dam, Sentola, never showed due to a knee injury as a yearling. Her progeny with Flyhawk were legendary—talented, hardy and elegant. The pairing of Flyhawk and Sentola was known as a "golden cross."

In 1945, the lovely Sentana was born, a miniature carbon copy of her dam with her coppery coat and blonde mane and tail. She was to be the last of the Flyhawk-Sentola mares and when she arrived at UConn, she and Sheba formed a strong broodmare foundation for the government bloodlines bred at the school.

Her foals were extraordinary individuals. A Panfield daughter, UC Pantana, was shown extensively by Willow Glen Morgans in California starting in 1964, and was a golden-maned beauty like her dam and sire. UC Pantana was also a successful broodmare and show horse; her trot was graceful, swift and light.

In 1965, UC Pantana won the English Championship at the Golden West National Morgan show, and in 1971, at the age of 16, she was the Reserve Champion in the English Pleasure division in Sacramento.

Sentana's sweet-tempered and athletic colt by Mentor, UC Senator, twice won the jumping class at the National Morgan Horse Show. Two of Sentana's daughters—full sisters by Panfield—UC Taffy and UC Sensation, went on to be top-producing broodmares for UConn.

In 1965, Sentana was purchased by her original breeder, Helen Greenwalt. Ms. Greenwalt bred her to the stallion, Windcrest Mr. Success, and the 1966 filly Glamadonna was the result.

The mare, still beautiful in her later years, was shown in a leadline class, a little girl named Sarah confidently astride her. Ever safe and trustworthy, the mare took excellent care of her young rider, and the pair won a large satin rosette that day.

Sentana was royalty, and her name still echoes in the annals of Morgan horse history.

UC Sensation

Panfield-Sentana
Born: 1958
University of Connecticut Top-Producing Broodmare from 1963-1978
Foals Produced: 11

A daughter of the perfect pairing of the magnificent stallion, Panfield, and the classic mare, Sentana, UC Sensation was a solid, typey mare with an eyelash-batting feminine face. She was a rich chestnut like her parents.

Sensation had 11 registered foals, including three full sisters by Windcrest Don Again: UC Donation in 1966, UC Fascination in 1967, and UC Flirtation in 1968. UC Donation, affectionately known as "Donut," was an amenable and athletic mare that went on to produce some winning foals of her own.

UC Sensation's loveliness lives on in the spirit of her descendants.

UC Melodie

Panfield-Sheba
Born: 1957
University of Connecticut Top-Producing Broodmare from 1961-1974
Foals Produced: 10

UC Melodie was a shining example of the golden cross of Panfield and Sheba. She was on the small side, a quick mover, and was popular with many students during her time at UConn.

She gave UConn ten foals, including the outstanding mares, UC Concertina and UC Lyric. Both of these mares contributed their exceptional qualities to the breeding and riding programs at UConn.

UC Melodie's daughter with Orland John Darling, UC Carillon, was used extensively as a saddle mount, and had one foal, UC Traveler, by Appevale Voyager. UC Traveler was popular in the riding program and is fondly remembered as an eager Drill Team horse, like his dam. A colt by Windcrest Don Again, UC Allegro, was English Pleasure World Champion in 1975.

UC Melodie demonstrated the versatility and refinement that is so prevalent in the Government bloodlines. Her contributions cemented UConn's broodmare foundation.

UC Melodie's strong influence continues to make itself seen in the present-day UConn breeding program.

UC Cannie

Canfied-Phillipa
Born: 1949
University of Connecticut Top-Producing Broodmare from 1954-1973
Foals Produced: 12

Somewhere...Somewhere in time's Own Space
There must be some sweet pastured place
Where creeks sing on and tall trees grow
Some Paradise where horses go,
For by the love that guides my pen
I know great horses live again.
~Stanley Harrison

Born in 1949 to the athletic and exquisitely feminine mare Phillipa and the stallion Canfield, "Cannie" possessed a brilliant chestnut coat and a small star on her face with a tiny smidge of a snip on her muzzle. Her eye was large and bright, her attitude kind and willing. She quickly became a favorite mare at the UConn Equine Program, and remained popular with the students for twenty years.

Cannie was also successful in the show ring. She was second in the Mare and Foal Class at the National Morgan Show in 1958, and she was Reserve Grand National Mare at the Eastern States Exposition in 1959. Her gaits, beauty and show presence made her a natural for the breeding and riding program at UConn.

As a UConn broodmare, UC Cannie produced the mares UC Electra, UC Expectation and UC Contessa. Her most famous foal was the flashy colt UC Marquis. UC Marquis became a successful show horse and a popular stallion, producing outstanding get.

Cannie, because of her personality and excellent conformation, was bred to many premier stallions including Mentor, The Explorer, Parade, and Windcrest Don Again.

Her last seven foals were colts, and thus, UConn was not able to acquire any of her mares in their herd. Cannie had 12 foals in total—9 of which were colts.

Cannie was a sturdy and healthy broodmare, and she was bred to the UConn herd stallion, Windcrest Don Again, for her final pregnancy in 1972. In the Spring of 1973, Cannie sported a swollen belly; days from delivering her foal. Her teats had not yet waxed, usually the telltale sign that a birth was imminent. Nothing was out of the ordinary as Cannie ate her dinner and settled in the roomy broodmare stall for the night.

The following morning, Anne Wiktor, an Animal Science major and student worker, arrived at the barn for the first feeding. As she approached the broodmare stall, Anne discovered Cannie stretched out in the bedding, her sides still with her lively newborn foal on top of her. Cannie had given birth to a chestnut colt in the early morning hours and had died, the kindness still apparent on her face.

Cannie's deep-red colt was healthy and active; bursting with eager life. However, if he didn't get his much-needed colostrum, his health would deteriorate quickly. Anne, her brain buzzing with urgency, ran to the phone to summon barn manager, Bruce Walters. Walters was at the barn in mere minutes.

Although hearts were broken over the loss of Cannie, grieving for the mare would have to come later. The situation at hand needed their prompt attention if the newborn foal was to survive—there would not be a second death that spring morning.

Anne and Bruce separated the colt from Cannie and brought him to a safe, quiet place as his dam's body was removed from the barn. The orphan was halter broken his first day of life as he didn't have a mother to follow and keep him safe. His human caretakers needed to lead him with ease. The mood of the barn was a somber one. Life, however, persevered as it stood before them on four tiny hooves.

There were no mares to foster the youngster, so Bruce Walters fashioned a nipple on a bucket and with Anne's help, they were able to teach the newborn foal to nurse. The colt suckled the life-giving formula with enthusiastic bliss, his little tail swishing and thumping at his sides. Later, they were able to acquire a proper nursing bottle from the cattle barn. The foal grew strong as Anne, barn staff and students took turns feeding him around the clock.

Anne named the colt UC Legacy.

The colt could not be turned out with the other mares and foals, so in order for Legacy to get his exercise, Anne had to hand walk the colt like a dog around UConn's Horsebarn Hill. Spectators on foot or in their cars would often stop to get a better look at the student and foal taking their lively walks around the barns and fields. Anne and Legacy bonded over these walks and as a result, the colt became friendly and cooperative with humans. His trust of people was unwavering; these two-legged creatures had saved his life and taken him into their hearts. Legacy grew to be a happy little chap that did not fear much.

At a mere five months old, UC Legacy was awarded a fifth place ribbon at the Morgan Regional Show in Northampton, Massachusetts. There were 15 mares and foals in the show that day and UC Legacy was the only orphan. Anne beamed with pride; her colt had done amazingly well and his future was a bright one. He was, after all, a son of the magnificent Windcrest Don Again.

At just under a year old, UC Legacy caught the attention of many a discerning horse person. He was a grand-looking colt with a polished, henna-toned coat and a spirited eye—he was meant for a show ring. UC Legacy was sold as a three-year-old to Pat Forst in San Jose, California, where he continued to touch hearts and thrill audiences. He was a prime example of the Morgan breed's versatility and was shown successfully in a variety of classes: Saddleseat, Pleasure Driving, Park Harness, In-Hand and Western.

A letter from Professor Nathan Hale to Pat Forst, dated November 26, 1976, expressed gratitude that UConn's charming orphan colt found a loving home:

> It is very nice to hear from you and find out that our UC Legacy is now located in California under your ownership. Legacy was the last foal that Cannie produced. In fact, she died during the foaling of Legacy and Legacy was brought up as an orphan foal fed on FOALAC for a period of 107 days consuming 772 quarts.

Pat Forst remembers "Leg" as a kind stallion that possessed patience and talent:

> Leg did anything you asked of him. He was more than a gentleman, the kids even groomed him and one time I saw a young gal walk right under him! He taught many how to ride.

UC Legacy was an outstanding sire as well, and he crossed well with the Fleetwing bloodlines. His most famous son was the four-time World Champion, Tico Valentino. Valentino's younger brother, Tico Fleetwood, was shown successfully on the West coast.

Anne Wiktor remembers UC Legacy with a great fondness and adoration, and it is clear that raising the foal was not just an everyday learning experience or college assignment for her. The bond between an orphan foal and a caregiver is strong and sure; time and distance do not weaken the ties or lessen the love—the connection grows more resolute with the passage of the years.

And, if you believe that there is such a place as Heaven, it is sure that Cannie and Legacy are together again in that place where our beloved horses go when their time on Earth is over. A place where a nuzzle and a nicker greet them and tall grasses brush gently against their knees.

In that peaceful, sun-touched pasture, mares can be with their foals again.

Cannie and Foal, 2012

UC Rhapsody

Panfield-Sheba
Born: 1958
University of Connecticut Top-Producing Broodmare from 1965-1979
Foals Produced: 9

*Rhapsody was a model of Morgan breed character and one of the most
admired mares over two decades at the UConn campus.* ~Dr Al Cowan,
Who's Who in New England Morgandom, NEMHA, 1987

UC Rhapsody had full-strength government Morgan in her impressive
pedigree. Her dam and sire came directly from the Government farm,
and they were outstanding examples of the high standards upheld by their
breeding program. Rhapsody was born in 1958, and was used extensively
in UConn's riding program. Her movements were thrilling and correct—a
spectacular example of a thoughtfully bred Morgan mare. Her dark chestnut
coat was deep and rich, and the only spot of white appeared on her face in
the form of a little teardrop star. She was breathtaking.

Her popularity as a riding horse kept her from being a mother until she was
seven years old. When she was bred, UC Rhapsody added splendor to the
UConn Morgan horse program from the outset. In 1965, her first foal came
into the world: a ravishing bay filly by Windcrest Don Again who was given
the regal name of UC Prima Dona. UC Prima Dona had an almost fawn-
like elegance; as fine and pretty as a porcelain teacup. UC Prima Dona was
purchased by Dr. Naseem Rauf of Massachusetts, and he showed her and
her offspring with great success.

In 1968, UC Rhapsody had a colt, a full brother to the spectacular UC Prima
Dona, UC Dark Shadow. UC Dark Shadow, also a dark chestnut like his dam,
became a favorite of Al Cowan's from the moment he came into the world.
As a yearling, he was already loaded with superstar presence—and Mabel
Owen of Merry Legs Farm in Dartmouth, Massachusetts was summarily
impressed. She was on the lookout for a young stallion, and when she saw
UC Dark Shadow, she looked no further and purchased the yearling colt
on the spot. UC Dark Shadow grew into a superb Morgan stallion bursting
with quality and energy—he showed successfully in Connecticut, Vermont,
Massachusetts and Granite State shows, winning Grand Champion In-Hand,
Park Harness Champion and Champion Park Saddle Horse titles. He was a
prodigious sire as well, with 34 colts and 32 fillies to his name.

Another filly, UC Contessa, by UC Marquis, was purchased by Roy and Janie Coats of Delhi, California. UC Contessa had a highly successful show career on the West coast, chalking up many Championships in Park Harness and In-Hand. UC Contessa's full sister, UC Electra, became a top-producing broodmare for UConn.

UC Rhapsody was a glorious mare that looked as if she was created by the paintbrush of a great master. She passed on her excellent qualities to her foals, and thus, we can still see the masterpiece that was UC Rhapsody today.

UC Expectation

The Explorer-UC Cannie
Born: 1961
University of Connecticut Top-Producing Broodmare from 1967-1976
Foals Produced: 6

She was versatile, had great babies and was a big chunky thing—classic Morgan type. ~Janice Callahan

UC Expectation was a dark chestnut mare that was popular as a lesson horse during her UConn tenure. She had a connected star and tapering strip on her alluring face, and was an excellent broodmare that carried on the outstanding qualities of her dam, Cannie. Her UConn foals include UC Athena, UC Predictor, and UC Cornucopia. Her pleasing nature won her many admirers.

Theresa Blatt purchased the 21-year-old mare and recalls her with adoration. "Exy" had a big neck and a broad back, and was, according to Theresa, "just the sweetest thing, like riding a sofa." Theresa also fondly remembers Exy as being the safest horse she ever encountered; nothing ever spooked her.

Exy was an easy breeder and was able to give Theresa two foals. She was such an easy breeder that on one occasion the hobbles, used on a mare's hind legs to prevent dangerous kicks to the stallion in the heat of the moment, weren't even necessary. One memorable day, she assertively pushed past Theresa and ran to the little hill where the stallion had been brought to her for the past three days. Exy stood on that hill to make it easier for Theresa's not-so-tall two-year-old stallion to mount. Exy knew what to do: when she got to her breeding spot, she pranced and stood at the ready for the young stud. She even called to him, "I'm reeeaaadyyyyy!", her nostrils fluttering with each seductive whinny. The young stallion was brought out and the breeding was quick and without incident.

Sadly, at 24, Exy injured herself in the field and was kindly put to sleep to end her pain. The gentle, trusting mare left behind many adoring friends and students.

Theresa Blatt, who now works exclusively with warmbloods, has not forgotten her kind and funny Morgan mare. And surely many more recall Exy's delightful personality and her quiet, yet effective lessons.

UC Taffy

Panfield-Sentana
Born: 1964
University of Connecticut Top-Producing Broodmare from 1972-1979
Foals Produced: 6

She has always had a good [foal]. ~Dr. Al Cowan, *Who's Who in New England Morgandom*, NEMHA, 1987

UC Taffy was a mare from the golden cross of the government Morgans Panfield and Sentana. She was a small, even-tempered chestnut mare with a blonde mane and tail, and she gave UConn six foals before she was sold to Peggy Clark of Salem, Connecticut in 1980. A good mother with her foals, Taffy could be reserved and introverted, and humans needed to earn her trust through patience and time. But, when that trust was formed, she could give a smooth and lovely ride. The mare could be spirited under saddle, and was sensitive to hard hands and stiff posture. A tight, anxious rider would soon learn to loosen up and learn to dance in time with Taffy's movements. Taffy was not an automatic horse, her riders learned to work for a level of true understanding in the saddle and she was a supreme teacher in this respect. One student recalled the day she was able ride Taffy correctly—light, balanced and in harmony. The student recalled that ride as a milestone, an epiphany in her equestrian education.

Taffy's foals include the aptly named UC Crackerjack, born in 1972, and the record-breaking yearling and future UConn broodmare, Salem Sentana. UC Crackerjack, by Windcrest Don Again, was Taffy's first colt, and he showed his Champion spirit as soon as his gangly legs grew strong and swift.

As a yearling in 1975, UC Crackerjack was sold to Roy and Janie Coats of California, and he went on to secure many Championships as a two-year old: he was either Junior Champion, Reserve Junior Champion, Grand Champion or Reserve Grand Champion in six of the seven shows he attended. UC Crackerjack kept getting better, and as a three-year-old he was Reserve Grand Champion at the California State Fair and at the Morgan Classic Royale. As a four-year-old, he was first in his class in six major shows. He cemented his superstar status when he was in the top ten at the Nationals in Oklahoma City. He didn't stop there. In 1977, at a mere five years old, UC Crackerjack was crowned Grand Champion Stallion at the Sierra, Morgan Medallion and California State Fair shows in addition to being High Point Stallion for the Northern California and Reserve High Point Stallion in Region 7.

With his long list of accolades and accomplishments, UC Crackerjack made his dam proud.

UC Taffy lived to an old age, and the success and excellence of her foals ensured that her proud legacy would live on.

She was one of the greats, a fine example of the Morgan breed.

UC Fascination
Windcrest Don Again-UC Sensation
Born: 1967
University of Connecticut Top-Producing Broodmare from 1974-1992
Foals Produced: 14

UC Fascination was one of our great mares. ~Dr. Al Cowan, Panel
Discussion, American Morgan Horse Association Meeting, Boston,
February, 1997

An exquisite coal-black mare, UC Fascination was born at UConn in 1967.
She possessed a doe-eyed femininity and eager, bold athleticism. And she
was a fertile mare, producing a total of 14 foals for UConn, including
UConn herd sire, the fiery UC Toronado. "Fas" was an incredible jumper
and could be a little hot and antsy, but she was never unreasonable. The more
experienced riders could channel her power into a thrilling, heart-pounding
ride. Hence, she was popular with many students in the riding program.
In 1977, UC Fascination was chosen along with UC Lyric to breed to the
supernaturally beautiful stallion, Waseeka's Showtime. The outside breeding
would introduce some new blood to the herd, and only the two best mares
at UConn had the privilege to potentially carry that honor. However, UC
Fascination did not get in foal with the Waseeka Farm stallion, but UC Lyric
did.

Although Fascination was not able to give a Waseeka's Showtime foal to
UConn, she contributed to the strength of the UConn Morgan breeding
program in another influential way: she crossed ideally with the Waseeka's
Showtime-UC Lyric colt, UC Ringmaster. She had seven quality foals with
UC Ringmaster including the incredible, crowd-pleasing Champions, UC
Merlin and UC Top Brass. Under the expert direction of Dr. James Dinger,
UC Fascination and UC Ringmaster produced UConn's first embryo transfer
foal, UC Wilde Mark, named after the student, Mark Wilde. Their filly, the
pretty chestnut UC Holiday, was born the same year as UC Wilde Mark and
became a top-producing broodmare for UConn—not to mention quite the
spirited lesson horse in the riding program. UC Holiday inherited her dam's
love of jumping and could also be a bit of an energetic gal.

Memories of Fas can elicit sighs of "oh, she was so beautiful" from the
alumni who remember her. Her delicate face, warm eyes and glowing, raven
coat—the image of UC Fascination is preserved in memories.

UC Concertina

Windcrest Don Again-UC Melodie
Born: 1966
University of Connecticut Top-Producing Broodmare from 1979-1991
Foals Produced: 6

"Connie" was a very nice girl, perfect for the riding program. She could do it all. ~John Bennett, Jr.

Picture a soft-eyed, golden mare with a relaxed Mona Lisa smile, happy perked ears and a friendly manner. That was the beloved UC Concertina.

UC Concertina, one of the "musical mares" by Windcrest Don Again, was a pretty chestnut that relished sailing over fences, the wind whistling in her upright ears. Her passion for jumping was rewarded with a Jumper Championship title at the National Morgan Show in Northampton, Massachusetts.

She is remembered as a sweetheart with a kind disposition and a generous nature; she was a wonderful riding horse and a patient teacher. "Connie" was a perfect beginner horse—steady, true and safe. As a broodmare, she produced talented and beautiful foals that went on to successful show careers, including the spectacular UC City Lights. She is the dam of UC Harry H, named after former UConn President Harry Hartley. Her daughters contributed their unique talents to the UConn riding program in addition to passing on her kind personality.

Many UConn alumni remember the chestnut mare with the congenial soul. They recall how she took care of them, her hooves firmly planted on the earth as they landed on her back, her legendary patience never wavering.

A leg swung over, and the student was safe in the saddle. Toes of boots found stirrup irons, and suddenly, flight was possible. Nervousness gave way to excitement. Tightness, in mind and body, melted away.

UC Concertina taught many how to live in the present and to leave their fears behind on the ground. For those timeless moments on Connie's back, they learned to let it all go. And just ride.

UC Concertina, 2012

UC Lyric

Windcrest Don Again-UC Melodie
Born: 1968
University of Connecticut Top-Producing Broodmare from 1974-1989
Foals Produced: 10

A grand lady. ~Dr. Al Cowan, *Who's Who in New England Morgandom*,
New England Morgan Association, 1987

If Elizabeth Taylor had been a Morgan mare, she would have been UC Lyric. A Windcrest Don Again "musical mare," UC Lyric possessed captivating eyes, talent, poise and a bombshell body with shapely legs. Lyric knew she was something special and could be somewhat aloof, but she was always gracious. If she could, she would have signed autographs with a smile and an elegant flourish of the quill.

UC Lyric was a bright, burnt sienna bay with a full and flowing mane, tail and foretop. Her undeniable excellence won her the Junior Champion title at the Connecticut Morgan Horse Show as a two-year-old.

Her first foal was the colt UC Acrobat, who went on to secure an impressive show record. Her first filly, UC Sonata, was touted as one of the best young mares at UConn—athletic, willing and sweetly feminine-looking. It's all about those eyes.

UC Lyric's most famous son is the Two-Time World Champion UC Ringmaster, "the best to hit the straw at UConn in a long time," according to Al Cowan. UC Ringmaster could easily be touted the most famous UConn-bred Morgan with his superior show record and scores of Champion offspring.

Careful and brilliant breeding can sometimes produce horses that have the ability to drop our jaws to the ground, gaping in silent astonishment. They are the horses that can send their competition scattering and shoot tingles through our marrow. The combination of Windcrest Don Again and his Upwey Ben Don blood, and that of UC Melodie, a mare that displayed the very best qualities of the Government-bred Panfield and Sheba, produced UC Lyric. It is no fluke that UC Lyric was the very picture of heart-stopping beauty and show-ready quality. And it is no surprise that her foals became stars themselves in the arena. One could almost see the flashbulbs popping when UC Lyric glided into view with the grace of a prima ballerina on opening night. With her delicately chiseled head, her strong legs, and her dished face with those alluring Hollywood starlet eyes—UC Lyric was simply…lovely.

UC Lyric, 2012

UC Electra

UC Marquis-UC Rhapsody
Born: 1975
University of Connecticut Top-Producing Broodmare from 1981-1990
Foals Produced: 4

She had show presence, was independent, and if you won her trust—she was
wonderful. ~Dr. Esther Noiles

UC Electra was a sparky little chestnut that could effectively teach a riding
student the importance of a quiet leg and soft hands. The mare could live up
to her name, and as Janice Callahan recalls, would "electrify" if her rider had
hard-yanking hands or all-over-the-place legs, kicking at her sides.

With a flash of her eye-whites and a bellow and snort through her wide
nostrils, the mare could be the very equine definition of "hot." What a sight
she must have been.

One could picture the student on her back being told by her prancing and
her head-tossing to relax and give.

Balance, be still, hands low, she seemed to say. Loosen the lower back. Sit
deep. Forget the final exams, the fight with your boyfriend, the homesickness,
the anxiety over late homework and full schedules. Release.

Then, and only then, would UC Electra turn into a willing dance partner,
moving with the grace of an impeccably-bred Morgan.

Learn to move with me, she said. As her student relaxed, Electra's eyes
softened and her neck arched gracefully as she filled the bridle with her
forward energy. Listen. Be. I will reward you with wings.

That's better, isn't it?

Merwin Black Beauty

Show Off's Right On-Fancy Hooker
Born: 1974
University of Connecticut Top-Producing Broodmare from 1980-1992
Foals Produced: 10

Merwin Black Beauty and two of her sons sired by UVM Trophy—Kirin and Shoki—were donated to UConn in 1980 by Dr. Johanna Shaw of Kent, Connecticut. Merwin Black Beauty was an attractive ebony mare that was a "great transmitter" according to Dr. Al Cowan—all of her foals were black. She was used in the riding program, and was fondly remembered as a mare with an abundance of personality.

Her foals with UC Ringmaster were exceptional individuals: UC Kiwi, UC Sundance, UC Phoebe and UC Centerfold. UC Centerfold was quite the looker, and she was kept in the UConn herd as a broodmare. As a two-year-old, Centerfold was Reserve Champion Mare at the Connecticut Amateur Morgan Show. She produced three foals for UConn.

"Beauty" crossed superbly with UC Ringmaster, so when UC Doc Daniels became a herd stallion, Beauty was bred to him as well. Their foals were also excellent: UC Doc's Image, UC Buckingham and UC Midnight Lace. UC Midnight Lace gave UConn some outstanding foals as well. "Lacey" has the distinction of being the mare of Kathy Pelletier's heart.

The mare is the heart and the soul of any successful breeding program, and Merwin Black Beauty made a strong contribution to the UConn herd and beyond.

UC Sonata

Ledgemere Bounty-UC Lyric
Born: 1977
University of Connecticut Top-Producing Broodmare from 1981-2000
Foals Produced: 8

She would do anything you asked of her. ~Kari Ameer

UC Sonata, 34 at the time of this writing, is quietly enjoying her retirement. Her legs are sound and clean, and she moves about without the clicks and snaps of old age. Her back is swayed slightly and her coat is a deep, reddish bay with muted dapples. She is beautiful, yes, but you don't get the full effect of that beauty until you see her face. It is exquisitely boned, feminine and fine, with huge, brown liquid eyes and a delicate muzzle. "She got her big eyes from her dam," Kari Ameer, UConn alumna, tells me.

Sonata now lives at the Ameer homestead with a friendly chestnut Thoroughbred named Pumpkin. On the day of my visit, Pumpkin noses me with a pocket-pony curiosity, but Sonata continues to graze, content to be by herself. I walk over to her and she allows me to touch her neck and run my hand over her shoulder. It is a privilege to be allowed into Sonata's world. She lifts her head for a few seconds, and my little digital camera snaps a picture just as she flicks her ears forward. Lucky shot.

Indeed, UC Lyric had those big, expressive eyes. You can even see them in Lyric's granddaughter, UC Ovation. It's the kind of eye that tells many stories of lessons, shows, ribbons and playful foals. Sonata's eyes peer right into my soul and take hold. I instantly adore her.

Kari tells me that UC Sonata "calls the shots," and I am not at all surprised. She has an energy that conveys confidence with a complete lack of fussiness and pretense. What you see is what you get with UC Sonata, and I can see why she was such a beloved mount in the UConn riding program. What a wonderful, effective teacher she must have been.

One alumna, Courtnay (Henninger) Lawrence, recalls a time when they were competing in a Saddleseat Equitation class, and the riders were told to drop their stirrup irons in a show trot. (Dropping the irons showcases a rider's true balance and skill—there are no stirrups to help support the rider in the saddle). As Courtnay removed her feet from the stirrups, one loosened iron softly grazed Sonata on her side. The mare, so well-trained and responsive, obediently proceeded with a perfect canter. Courtnay quickly collected Sonata and brought her back to a trot, and the pair earned a second place ribbon.

Indeed, Sonata would do anything you asked of her.

Trainer and rider Jennifer (Gregson) Backs had her first hunter trial on UC Sonata and remembers "having a blast." Another alumna, Lynn Babbitt, won the English Pleasure Championship with Sonata at the Connecticut Morgan Horse Association amateur show in 1986. A photo from that memorable day clearly shows a beaming Lynn and a flashy Sonata, ears perked and eyes bright—a red, blue and gold rosette fluttering from her bridle. A video of Sonata from that time clearly depicts a forward-moving, high-stepping, go-getter of a Morgan mare. The arena was her stage and she was the star. Lynn recalls that the hand gallop was her favorite part. The mare just loved to go, go, go.

Lynn recalls:

> She caught my eye...I had any horse there [UConn] at my disposal to ride—even the stallions we were using in the research program—but she had such a sparkle in her eye, I chose her. I had grown up showing my own Morgan and missed an opportunity then to be in the show ring, and I knew Sonata would be great.

Sonata was a fantastic broodmare and had many gorgeous, plump babies that went on to accomplish great things. Even her accidental pregnancy, the result of a loose warmblood, was a success. That surprise foal was spotted years later at a dressage clinic.

In retirement, the mare was still full of her go-getter spirit, and Kari entered a hunter pace with her. The 26-year-old Sonata, ever the jump-lover, sailed over 80% of the fences on the course. She barely huffed and puffed after the exciting ride, and horses younger than she were drenched in sweat and were quite done for the day, thank you. Sonata seemed to say, "well, now that the warm-up is done, which way to the real show?"

Today, she puts her ears up straight when she sees her favorite person, Dana—Kari's mother. Dana's light and love is the graying bay mare in the back pasture. She is allowed into Sonata's world daily, and the honor never loses its wonder. Sonata gets her share of soft peppermints, and life for the mare has taken on an easy, peaceful air. UC Sonata's big eyes still have that unmistakable sparkle—and they will always remind you of who she is: a legend.

Addendum

UC Sonata passed away about three months after this chapter was written. She was surrounded by love as she took her final journey...

A few days after Sonata's passing, I went on a bike ride to reminisce about good times. I remembered how I used to take Sonata out on the rail trail and surrounding roads on a retractable dog leash- she and I would go jogging together. She loved it.... though I was obviously not quite fast enough for her, but she didn't mind. She got to explore and see the world a bit without someone on her back. I saw a couple of her favorite fields that we had the privilege to ride through at certain times of the year. In the spring I would ride her out there and enjoy the peace and quiet, while she munched on the new grass. In the fall, once the corn was down, we could canter around the edge of the fields, taking in the fresh autumnal air and gorgeous New England fall colors. We will miss her everyday, but her spirit will never leave us.
UC Sonata, May 2, 1977- August 21, 2011.

~Kari Ameer

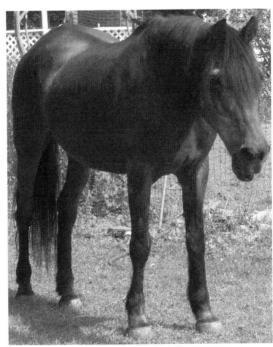

UC Sonata, 2011

Delmaytion Desire

Corinth Renaissance-Delmaytion Dolly
Born: 1975
University of Connecticut Top-Producing Broodmare from 1980-1998
Foals Produced: 10

She was a true testament to the Morgan versatility and temperament.
~Megan (Chapman) Thompson

January 2010: Delmaytion Desire, known simply as "Desire," passed away at age 35. The golden mare lived out her retirement with Dr. Sandra Bushmich, large animal veterinarian and UConn pathobiology professor, and her daughter, Aurora. Desire was a much-loved family member, and she brought joy to many during her full life at UConn and beyond. She contributed to the rich history of the UConn area: two of her children, UC Daybreak and UC Serendipity, belong to two of the oldest families of the Mansfield and Storrs, Connecticut community—the Stearns and Thompsons, respectively.

She was a soft-eyed beauty with a thin stripe of white on her face, and she emanated patience and calm. She was the type of horse that could ignite the first flickers of horse-craziness in children. For the grown-ups, she would evoke memories of favorite school ponies of long ago. She was, for many, a Horse of Dreams.

She came to UConn as a yearling, and Janice Callahan recalls her thusly:

She was the best of the best as far as school horses go. She could teach any level, any rider. The kids loved her—she was sweet, forgiving. She was also compact and had lots of personality.

UConn alumna Megan (Chapman) Thompson recalls Desire to have been wonderfully versatile and reliable as well:

She was calm, steady—gentle enough for the beginner riders, but athletic, willing and talented enough to be a favored mount of the advanced students.

Desire seemed to be just the perfect horse, pleasant-mannered and kind— but with a show horse's spirit. She was the mount of choice for the Drill Team and was a standout athlete on the eventing team as well. In 1990, she won Reserve Champion Open Working Hunter at the New England Morgan

101

Horse Show. As a broodmare, she had lovely babies and was an attentive mother, her face an equine display of maternal pride. Her outstanding progeny include the Champion by UC Ringmaster, UC Town Crier; UC Arthur L; UC Last Tango; and UC Curtain Call.

Drill Team member Timothy Budris recalls her "saving" him; she never hesitated at the fences. He recalled her as a "push-button" horse with legendary steadfastness and poise.

Horses are horses, however—and even Desire could be prone to a bad day: Timothy was riding Desire in a lesson, and the normally gentle mare was extremely cranky, kicking out at horses passing her in the arena. She even bucked a few times and nearly unseated Timothy, who was growing more baffled by the minute. Then, the ever-reliable mare pulled a first: she stopped at a jump, sending Timothy sailing over her neck and into the dirt. Timothy got up, dusted himself off and wiped the arena grit from his face. He wobbled out of the arena with the grumpy mare in tow. His push-button mount seemed to have a bee in her bonnet today—perhaps a whole angry hive. Timothy could not understand why Desire had been so uncharacteristically naughty. Then, as if the Universe had read his befuddled mind, his answer came. John Bennett approached Timothy and Desire as they exited the arena.

"Oh, there she is, I'll take her," Bennett said, calm as can be, taking the reins from Timothy's hands.

Curious, Timothy watched as Bennett removed her saddle and took her around the corner where a handler had a stallion in-hand, waiting. In an instant, Desire was bred to the stallion.

Timothy watched in amazement, and started laughing to himself. He immediately forgave her in his heart for her isolated bad behavior—she was in heat. He felt a wave of relief wash over him. That one crazy ride was equine nature at work.

In 1998, Desire was frequently coming up lame in the lesson program. At 22, she needed to transition out of the school and to enjoy the life of a backyard horse, lazily exploring trails and munching apple chunks left in her feed tub. John Bennett adored the mare and wanted to find the perfect retirement home for her, where she could be loved and pampered.

He remembered Dr. Sandra Bushmich mentioning that she wanted to find a safe horse for her daughter, Aurora, a middle-school student at the time. Now, Bennett was on a mission to get Delmaytion Desire into Sandy's heart.

He discussed Desire with her, explaining that she would be the perfect horse for Aurora.

John Bennett could be persuasive, especially when he knew what was best for his horses. Since he was a consummate horseman, his words were listened to by anyone looking to acquire an equine family member. He told Sandy he could arrange for the mare to be shod, and to be transported right to Sandy's home. Bennett explained that with the correct shoes and light riding, Desire would be sound in no time.

Sandy explained, "It was hard for me to refuse. He guaranteed she'd be sound, and he was right. She was a wonderful horse. She was ideal for my daughter."

It was a perfect match.

Desire proved to be an easy-keeper with rock-hard feet, and she and Aurora quickly became best friends. Desire's popularity never waned: the affable mare delighted children by giving pony rides at birthday parties and could be seen bedecked in ribbons at the Mansfield Middle School Medieval Fair. She was bombproof, but not a plug—as safe as they come, but with a merry glimmer in her eye.

In 2007, Sandy received an urgent call from her husband and said the words no horse owner ever wants to hear: he told her that Desire was dead. Sandy, who worked close to home, raced to be with her mare. When she arrived, she found Desire lying on her side in some deep, soft mud in her paddock. The mare did not stir. Sandy felt a leaden weight forming in her gut. It was dread.

Was her mare gone?

Sandy went to Desire, knelt down close to her face, and put a comforting hand on her golden neck. She whispered softly into the mare's downy ear:

Desire, do you want to live?

An ear flicked ever-so-slightly in response.

Desire seemed to wake from a deep sleep, moved by the familiar and safe sound of Sandy's voice. She proceeded to lift her head out of the muck and stand up, her limbs shaking. Sandy tended to her and administered some medication to relieve her discomfort. She ascertained that her mare had colicked.

She fully recovered that day, but in subsequent winters, she continued to concern her family. She would frighten her loving humans, then make a miraculous last-minute recovery. One day, her family even called out the backhoe man, their hearts heavy with the sad truth that they needed to give their sweet old girl eternal sleep to ease her pain. Desire took one look at that backhoe and decided to perk up and eat. *Not today*, she seemed to say.

When Desire's strong heart stopped beating, it did so well before the dreaded backhoe man arrived. Desire did not want to see him and his big, yellow machine—she wanted to go on her own terms, with grace, with dignity and with her family beside her.

Delmaytion Desire, the Horse of Dreams, taught important lessons to many in her lifetime: we are here to be true to ourselves, to teach, to learn. To love.

Delmaytion Desire, *circa* 1992

UC Esther

UC Ringmaster-UC Electra
Born: 1985
University of Connecticut Top-Producing Broodmare from 1993-2002
Foals Produced: 5

She was a pretty girl with big eyes. She was a great lesson horse. ~John
Bennett, Jr.

UC Esther, a lovely,
long-legged mare, was a
burnished liver chestnut
like her dam, UC Electra.
Her large, dark eyes were
gentle and kind.

UC Esther was named after
Dr. James Dinger's grad
student, Esther Noiles.
Esther remembered she
had a migraine headache
the day that she and Dr.
Dinger were looking

UC Esther, *circa* 1993

over a field of new foals. Dr. Dinger spotted the dark filly and proclaimed,
"We'll name this one Esther." The kind gesture helped her to forget the
dull, constant throbbing in her head. Esther recalled her young namesake
filly was a "very pretty foal." UC Esther grew to be a tall mare with a slim
build—she looked almost like a Thoroughbred. She had two white socks on
her hind feet and an elongated star on her forehead. She joined the UConn
top-producing broodmare band in 1993 when she foaled her first filly, UC
Three Times a Lady. Her most famous daughter was a beauty by the name of
UC Irish Rhapsody, a chestnut by UC Toronado. In 2002, she retired from
her broodmare and lesson career at UConn and moved to Tennessee, where
she was no doubt adored and treasured. The slender mare with the huge eyes
touched many lives during her time in the rolling emerald hills of UConn.

Song of Courage

Courage of Equinox-UC Taffy
Born: 1986
University of Connecticut Top-Producing Broodmare from 1994-2005
Foals Produced: 7

A full sister to the record-breaking mare, Salem Sentana, Song of Courage was a beautiful liver chestnut with impeccable bloodlines. Her sire was Courage of Equinox, and her dam was the strongly Government-influenced chestnut mare, UC Taffy.

Song of Courage, because of her stellar pedigree, was used mostly in the breeding program at UConn, and she produced some splendid foals for the school. They include UC Hope and Courage, UC Courage Under Fire and UC Tee Time, all great mares in their own right. Janice Callahan fondly remembers the mare UC Tee Time as a beloved favorite amongst the students in the riding program. "She would do anything, was sweet as can be and was really cute," Callahan recalls. "Great school horse for anyone." Tee Time is also the dam of current UConn junior stallion, the bay champion, UC Doc Sanchez.

In 2002, Song of Courage was sold and moved to central Massachusetts. The beauty and talent of her sparkling pedigree are readily seen in the current-day Morgan horses at UConn.

Song of Courage, 2012

UC Aria

Entertainer-UC Lyric
Born: 1987
University of Connecticut Top-Producing Broodmare from 1994-2006
Foals Produced: 7

Short, strong, compact and game. Put her at a jump at any angle and she'd get it done. ~Mary O'Donovan

A weathered-penny chestnut, UC Aria was a treasured lesson program horse, Drill Team mount and top-producing broodmare for UConn. Her offspring include UC Ariel, UC Olympic Star, UC Crescendo, UC Mr. T's Destiny, UC Aries, UC Lyre and a junior herd stallion, UC Domination.

UC Aria's gentle and accommodating nature earned her the nickname of "Grandma," but she was no slouch when faced with a jump. She would leap over the rails like a cricket, land, collect herself, snort and look eagerly for her next fence. She was a fun ride with her endless energy, and she was an absolute joy in the barn, happily trilling and nickering to passersby.

When retirement drew near for Aria, Kathy Pelletier hatched an elaborate plan to get the mare to her farm in time for her daughter Courtney's birthday. Courtney Pelletier adored Aria and was bordering on despondent that her beloved mare was featured in the upcoming horse sale and auction at UConn.

Kathy made sure that Aria was hers at the sale, but did not let Courtney know that she had made that happen. Courtney thought her favorite mare was sold and gone forever.

While attending a Future Farmers of America banquet, Kathy claimed she needed to leave as she'd just received a call that one of her mares, Salem Sentana, had a fever. She told Courtney she had to leave at once to tend to the ailing horse, and that she'd meet her back home. This was all untrue, however—Kathy was meeting her friend, Carolyn Stearns, who was transporting Aria to the Pelletier farm. When Kathy arrived home, the horse trailer containing the mare arrived minutes after. They had to move quickly and get Aria off the trailer and into a stall, the banquet would soon be over and Courtney would be on her way home.

When Courtney Pelletier arrived home, she ran to Salem's stall to check on her condition. Salem was chewing on some hay and seemed relaxed and comfortable. She was a picture of health and vitality with not a sign of fever or a drop of sweat on her coat. Salem Sentana briefly lifted her head and looked at Courtney as if to ask, "what are you so worried about?" The mare then lowered her head and nonchalantly returned to her hay.

What was going on?, Courtney wondered.

Confusion gave way to jittery excitement as the realization washed over her:

You have Aria here, don't you?

The air was still in the Pelletier barn, and a familiar, comforting sound reached Courtney's ears: Aria was talking to her. The birthday surprise was in her new stall, gleefully whuffling to her favorite human. Courtney audibly gasped.

Aria!

It isn't every day that a young woman can possess her one special horse. Horse and human may brush by each other in life, share a friendship, and, all too soon, the moment is gone. The young woman will grow up, graduate from school, find a career, and perhaps raise a family. Years will pass. However, that one horse never leaves her memory—and every subsequent horse she meets is compared to that one she met long ago, the one that *connected*.

UC Aria is that special, unforgettable horse, her lessons woven into the fabric of many lives.

UC Ovation

Otterbrook Jubilee-UC Sonata
Born: 1990
University of Connecticut Top-Producing Broodmare from 1997-2006
Foals Produced: 4

A real sweetheart. ~Janice Callahan, Instructor and Coach of the
UConn Equestrian Team, 1976-2006

UC Ovation, a stocky dark bay mare with large, loving eyes, was a favorite mount during her time at UConn. A gentle peach, she was the horse of choice for the beginner rider in UConn's lesson program.

UConn alumna, Julie Biron, had the pleasure of training Ovation as a yearling as part of Horse Appreciation with Janice Callahan, Instructor and Coach of the UConn Equestrian Team. Julie taught Ovation how to trailer, park out and lead properly—and her equine student learned tasks quickly and willingly. Ovation and Julie readily demonstrated their trust of each other and they were an outstanding team because of it: in 1991, they won First Place In-Hand at the Little International Horse Show at UConn.

The young Ovation showed her good mind and reliability very early on. The sensible mare marched in her first UConn parade at age three and she was a perfect, quiet angel the whole time. Her pleasing personality earned her the nickname of "Marshmallow."

UC Ovation was the result of an outside breeding in the interest of adding a versatile riding horse to the UConn Morgan herd. UC Sonata was bred to the dark bay stallion, Otterbrook Jubilee, and UConn received their wish: as a riding horse, Ovation was as versatile as they come. She taught hunt seat and jumping and was a hands-down favorite for beginner Western. She possessed patience beyond her years and she could be seen trotting steadily and safely with a novice rider on her back. She had the ability to sense if the rider was nervous and she wouldn't run off or toss her head impatiently if the reins were inadvertently pulled. If a rider had more experience, Ovation would size them up and offer more of a challenge by getting a little sassy. Her attitude was never unsafe or naughty; she just wanted to give a good ride to anyone who swung a leg over her. She had a classic sturdy Morgan build with "a back like a couch and legs like tree trunks," according to one student who rode her. Everyone loved her.

109

UC Ovation was easy to get in foal, but often lost, or "slipped," the fetus as her pregnancy progressed. A hormone regimen was assigned to the mare once she was confirmed in foal and this proved to be an effective solution. "Mama O" went on to produce many bold and beautiful babies for the UConn breeding program. As a mother, she was patient and kind; she was a mare that truly enjoyed motherhood.

UC Emma and UC Applause, two of Ovation's notable daughters, became broodmares in the UConn herd, and they perpetuated Ovation's unique brand of reliability.

At UConn, Ovation was an easy keeper who loved her carrots, apples and bran mash with molasses, and keeping weight on the mare was never a problem.

When Mama O's breeding and lesson days were over, she was offered for sale at the UConn Horse Sale and Auction. Kristen, an alumna of the school and a fan of the lovely mare, outbid everyone that day to obtain the horse of her heart. Ever popular, the 20-year-old mare received the most bids, and she was the top-priced horse of the day.

When the auctioneer rambled off the name of the new owner of the beloved Mama O, Kristen couldn't understand the garbled words over the PA system. She turned to her best friend who had accompanied her and asked, "did I get her?"

The answer was yes. Kristen, upon learning that Ovation was hers, suddenly felt weak in her legs and had to kneel on the ground. Overcome with joyful emotion, she could barely see through happy tears to write the check to take her home; her best friend came to the rescue again by filling out the amount so all that Kristen needed to do was sign. It was truly a dream come true, now Kristen could simply "look out her window and see Ovation every day."

Today, UC Ovation continues to demonstrate her incredible versatility. Ovation and Kristen ride sidesaddle, an equestrian art where both of the rider's legs are on one side of the horse. Ovation is still ridden in a thick eggbutt snaffle bit, ever reliable and safe. She recently carried a four-year-old boy in his first leadline class and was gentle and motherly with her young charge. In her paddock, she enjoys a retirement fit for a benevolent Queen, and she moves about gracefully, in no hurry. Under the soft, muted light of the late afternoon sunshine, you can see shadows of the dapples on her flanks. She flutters her nostrils to catch the clover-scented air and after a good whiff, she lowers her head to graze on the grass and dandelions all around her. Healthy and happy, her coat shines like polished mahogany. UC Ovation, Mama O, is home.

UC Ovation, 2010

UC Carberry

Townshend Melarry-UC Topaz
Born: 1989
University of Connecticut Top-Producing Broodmare from 1995-2001
Foals Produced: 6

She's an easy horse to handle and a great broodmare. ~John Bennett, Jr.

Although officially listed in the American Morgan Horse Registry as a brown, UC Carberry is coal-black with no white markings. Her dam was the athletic chestnut UC Topaz and her sire was a dark, handsome knight, Townshend Melarry. She was named after the UConn student who assisted with her foaling, Cheryl Carberry.

Almost all of Carberry's foals were deep black, and they sold quickly. One of her daughters with UC Toronado, UC Cadberry, was a Reserve Champion in Carriage Driving at the Vermont Spring Classic. She's a smart and pretty mover—and in the words of her proud owner, Linda Roto—a real "pocket pony."

Other UC Carberry progeny include UC Moonshadow, UC Black Razberry, UC Blackberry, UC Mayberry and UC Huckleberry.

UC Topaz

Ledgemere Bounty-UC Donation
Born: 1977
Foals Produced: 3

A lively chestnut with a wonderful personality, John Bennett recalls that UC Topaz could be somewhat difficult to breed. She is worth noting because she made a lasting and influential contribution to the UConn breeding program through her daughter, UC Carberry, and her son, the legendary UC Doc Daniels.

An athletic mare, Topaz did well as a hunter/jumper, a trait she inherited from her dam, UC Donation. Topaz was not high-headed and could really point herself over the fences and fly.

Her sturdiness, energy and talent can still be seen in UConn's junior stallions, UC Doc Sanchez and UC Domination—two bay sons by her famous and handsome colt, UC Doc Daniels.

UC Hope and Courage

UC Toronado-Song of Courage
Born: 1994
University of Connecticut Top-Producing Broodmare from 1999-2003
Foals Produced: 4

She was a beautiful girl. So much fun to ride. Clever, comfortable, soft and really talented. ~Megan (Heffley) Brauch

UC Hope and Courage was a glossy black, like her sire, and she could also be just as hot-blooded. She had large, wide-set eyes and a gorgeous, feminine face that was undeniably Morgan.

She showed her resiliency and fighting spirit very early on in her life: as a weanling, she rolled under a fence, probably in an attempt to get some out-of-reach grass—and as she pulled herself out, she fractured her shoulder. The black filly's future, once filled with promise and spark, suddenly darkened and became still.

The on-call vet was summoned, and he vowed to save the filly. A student tending Hope remembered the determined doctor as saying, "I can't put down a horse named Hope and Courage." The filly was spared an all-too-early death and was promptly given stall rest as she healed.

Months would pass, and boredom must have gripped her, but she never gave in to a bad attitude or despair. One of her biggest fans, Nancy Tomastik, would visit the filly every week—and Hope enjoyed those times immensely. Each time Nancy would approach her stall, Hope would nicker and perk her lovely little ears forward. The visits revealed a kind, endearing horse—soulful, empathic and aware. Nancy remembers how Hope would lean into her and nuzzle the stall bars to get close to her. The smoldering jewel was burnished to show a gentle inner nature.

When her shoulder healed, she was allowed to play again. In her first turnout since her injury, she didn't bolt away and fly into the fences and re-injure herself. She was very deliberate and careful—and it was those qualities that eventually made her a nurturing mother to her foals.

Student Mary O'Donovan assisted John Bennett with Hope's early training, and recalls how the filly would "tuck in her tail and buck" like a wildcat. It

114

took nearly a full year for her to stop that behavior, but Hope always had a spark. She was her sire's daughter. John Bennett never gave up on the young mare, and eventually Hope learned to engage her hindquarters and float like a dressage horse.

At three, she was saddled and ridden. The bucking had long ceased, but she had discovered a new and dangerous habit—rearing. She was like a shooting star that had been trapped in a net, and the rearing could keep her from having a career as a lesson horse. She was then assigned to student Megan Heffley (now Brauch) as an Independent Study. Megan's job was to give Hope some specialized attention and dressage training so she could possibly enter the equine program as a school horse. Megan soon discovered the mare to be exceptionally sweet, but a hot ticket that needed a patient, understanding hand. Hope could get flustered and confused—and she would leap up with her front legs to express her frustration. Megan's persistence and quiet leadership soon showed Hope what was expected of her, and the willing-to-please mare was transformed into a soft, responsive riding horse, her boundless energy now directed into her forward, cloud-like gaits.

As a broodmare, Hope had outstanding babies, and was a favorite in the barn because of her people-loving personality.

Days of sunshine and nursing foals filled Hope's days. The mare had escaped an untimely death, and it seemed sure that she would enjoy many years with the people she loved, the wind ruffling her wavy foretop as she grazed in her turnout with a fat, happy foal at her side. But it was not to be. As a ten-year-old, the mare's condition deteriorated rapidly; she lost weight and her gleaming black coat dulled. No one knew the reason for her sudden decline—vets and staff were equally puzzled. The mare's eyes, once so radiant and friendly, filled with worry and confusion.

One heartbreaking day, it was obvious to her caregivers that Hope was in extreme discomfort, and the vet was called in again. This time, the beautiful black mare could not be saved. The final kindness was given to her quickly and painlessly. Hope had given way to courage as the mare embarked on her final journey, surrounded by love.

Soon after, Nancy Tomastik visited the UConn barns, and did not see her favorite mare. She found John Bennett walking the barn aisles, and she inquired about Hope. Bennett informed Nancy that the mare had been released from her mysterious agony and was finally at peace.

Nancy immediately felt the sting of tears well up in her eyes, and she had no choice but to let them fall over her cheeks. The great mare, her Black Beauty, was gone.

The cause of Hope's illness was never discovered; it remains a mystery to this day.

UC Hope and Courage certainly lived up to her name. Something in that filly's glowing eyes must have indicated bravery, promise and stoicism. She passed on her exceptional qualities to her foals—including the heroic UC High Hopes, "'Shoe." Shoe was also horribly injured from a paddock accident, acquiring multiple fractures in both of his hind legs. The brave little chestnut horse not only survived, but he healed completely and became a dressage Champion. He is truly his mother's son. His amazing story is featured earlier in this book.

To UC Hope and Courage: your time with us was too short, but your black flame blazes on in the memories of the many who adored you. May you forever have acres of green fields under your hooves.

UC Holiday

UC Ringmaster-UC Fascination
Born:1985
University of Connecticut Top-Producing Broodmare from 1996-2003
Foals Produced: 7

I trust her more than any other horse I've ever met.
~Jaclyn (Gallant) Gagnon, owner

UC Holiday looks like a little girl's horse dream. Her coat glows like polished copper and her crooked blaze is reminiscent of a splash of white paint dripping down a barn door. Her friendly, open face is inquisitive as she nuzzles coat pockets, searching for treats.

Her story at UConn involves many students who rode her and learned from her. John Bennett recalls the young UC Holiday as a challenging horse to train, and called her a lively little thing that would "leap around all over" the arena. The filly squarely landed on a fence during one memorable bouncy episode.

Holiday truly enjoyed sailing over jumps, ears forward and eyes wide. She could really move out and show her enthusiasm and energy—she was known around the barn as the hot little mare with loads of firepower. When she really got moving, her nostrils would flare and burn red as she ate up the ground with each surefooted step.

Holiday barely touched the tape at 15 hands, but she had a heart as big as UConn itself. Her ground manners were impeccable; she was always a perfect lady when her hooves were picked out and her coat curried and brushed. She was a wonderfully effective equine teacher as she taught her students how to sit balanced in the saddle and to not pull back on the reins in order to gain a better seat and position. She was quick to communicate to any hard-handed rider that if they jerked and leaned on her mouth, it would only make her pull harder. Holiday could give a rein-yanking student quite an exciting ride—and the student would think better of it next time.

During one riding lesson, the notoriously energetic Holiday spooked when the girth loosened around her ribs, and she exited the riding arena with the saddle slipping from her back. The rider dismounted unscathed, but the little mare's natural flight instinct went into overdrive, and in her attempted escape, she managed to rip a tendon in her foreleg, right to the bone. Three months of cleaning and dressing the wound under the caring and skilled hands of assistant barn manager, Kathy Pelletier, healed her so immaculately that she did not show the slightest limp in her step. Once again, the UConn Morgan horse exhibited resiliency and toughness that was befitting of a horse bred for the mounted army.

UC Holiday was a good mother and foaled out with ease. Kathy Pelletier described her as a "very spirited horse that had beautiful babies."

She wasn't an overprotective mare, and her foals learned confidence from her. She was careful with her babies and was always mindful of where they were; when she foaled, Holiday would deliberately position her legs and twist her body to avoid stepping on her newborn.

As part of an Independent Study with Horse Unit Supervisor John Bennett, UConn student Julie Biron trained the mare to drive as a pair with her full brother, UC Wilde Mark, UConn's first embryo transfer horse. The two chestnut progeny of UC Ringmaster and UC Fascination looked like gleaming chestnut bookends as they effortlessly pulled a carriage, often trotting in unison. The siblings were not only beautiful, but also cool in the face of potential disaster. One day, while Bennett and Julie were driving the team, a horse gave in to its flight instinct while hitched to its cart, got loose and started galloping around the barns, dragging a tire behind him.

Bennett leaned over to Julie and said in a calm but somewhat ominous tone, "Get ready to bail."

Julie did not need to be told twice—she jumped out of the rig to prepare for the possibility of the two horses becoming panicked by the free horse that was now wide-eyed and snorting as it tried to flee from the tire. The horse came close to the harnessed team, but Holiday and Mark stayed put—only prancing a little in response to the excitement. There was no runaway cart that day: Holiday and Mark focused on John Bennett, who confidently held the reins and transmitted his calm energy through the leather to the metal bits in their mouths. Julie was astounded and impressed, the two horses had exhibited poise and composure in a dangerous situation.

The loose horse eventually came to stop and was caught. The animal was miraculously unharmed.

UC Holiday was the preferred mount of student Jaclyn Gallant. Jaclyn, an alumna of the UConn equestrian team, always picked UC Holiday when she was given the choice of a horse for lessons and equestrian team events during her time at the University. They clicked immediately.

UC Holiday and Jaclyn Gagnon sail over a fence, 2008

Holiday, despite her fence mishaps in her youth, truly enjoyed jumping and her eyes would light up when she saw a lesson ring full of fences.

"Holiday had a little saddle seat horse attitude," Jaclyn described her, "and she absolutely loved to jump."

Jaclyn was present for the birth of her beloved Holiday's last foal, UC Celebration.

"I almost missed it," Jaclyn laughed. "She knew what she was doing and by the time I got there, her foal was nearly out!"

Years later, when Holiday reached retirement age, Jaclyn was able to acquire the mare and give her a forever home.

Holiday's strong maternal instinct transferred to members of her non-equine family. One Christmas, Jaclyn's husband gifted her with a tiny Jack Russell puppy. Holiday instantly demonstrated her trustworthy nature with the diminutive pup. The rascal would run after Holiday and Jaclyn as they rode in the arena, and would chase the mare's tail. Holiday was protective of the puppy, and never kicked out at him. She stopped on a dime and stood stock

119

still when the puppy was near, and even contorted herself so she wouldn't step on him—just as she did with her foals. Holiday even allowed the little dog to eat out of a tub with her.

As a member of a large herd, Jaclyn described Holiday as the one that stayed out of trouble and steered clear of conflict. She never fought for alpha status; instead, she was quite content to keep to her herself.

Today, she still has that great sense of self-preservation and she is an easy-keeper, distinct traits of the Government-bred Morgan. Her hooves are free of steel and only recently she was given a quilted blanket for the bitterly cold winter days.

Jaclyn Gallant, now Jaclyn Gagnon, recalls the day she brought Holiday home as one of the best days of her life. Holiday and Jaclyn still enjoy their rides together, and they know each other like best friends. It is a real-life fairytale of a girl and her horse.

Salem Sentana

Courage of Equinox-UC Taffy
Born: 1983
University of Connecticut Top-Producing Broodmare from 1991-2003
Foals Produced: 4

She was very nice to get along with, a nice athletic mare. A very sweet horse.
~Peggy (Clark) Alderman

Salem Sentana was born in 1983 to the prolific black chestnut stallion, Courage of Equinox, and the lovely chestnut and blonde UConn-bred mare, UC Taffy. The combination of colors from her dam and sire made for a striking, uniquely-colored filly: Salem Sentana had a rich, almost liver chestnut coat and a silky flaxen tail. Her face had two spots of white—a star between her eyes and an abbreviated blaze above her finely tapered muzzle. It was hard to find flaw in Salem Sentana. She had a powerful shoulder and neck, sound legs, a refined and lovely face, and gossamer, flowing gaits.

Peggy Clark of Salem Farm bred and raised the filly, and when Salem was sold in Northampton, Massachusetts, she sold for the incredible price of $25,000—the highest price ever paid for a yearling at public auction. One could imagine the jaws that dropped when Salem entered the auction ring that day, a heated bidding war building in intensity. Salem Sentana had arrived.

Her buyer, noted Connecticut architect, Murray Gibson, could see the potential in the young beauty, and under his skillful care Salem was awarded the World Champion yearling filly title in Oklahoma City.

Salem Sentana was without imperfection with her strong Government bloodlines, making her a natural for a Morgan breeding program. She returned to UConn to begin her broodmare and riding program career, and many alumni remember her with great fondness. "Sweet" was a common adjective.

Salem was a willing mare, as steady as they come. She was a reliable UConn Drill Team member and a wonderful lesson horse—she could anticipate what needed to be done long before students could organize themselves in the saddle. She was an excellent teacher and would perform her job well, and as result, many learned how to ride in balance and to form a true partnership with their mount.

An alumna remembers a time when she observed a fellow student growing frustrated in a jumping lesson when Salem was rushing the fences. Janice Callahan, riding instructor and equestrian team coach, urged the student to slow Salem down between fences, offering suggestions for her leg, seat and hand aids. The student exclaimed that it was impossible because Salem "just wouldn't listen." However, Salem *was* listening, but she wouldn't give out free passes. A rider had to learn to ask the right questions to get the desired result from her. Janice asked the student to dismount, got on Salem's back, and rode the mare through the jump course perfectly. The student no doubt learned a valuable lesson from Salem that day: riding can sometimes test one's patience to its limits, and a horse can teach us to step back and reorganize, be in the now, sit up straight and ride with confidence and balance.

However, the frustrating moments are worth all the tooth-grinding and anxiety—it is a wonderful feeling when it all comes together with harmony and connection. It is then that the ride becomes a graceful dance.

Salem Sentana gave many that feeling.

Salem had numerous fans and admirers, including the singer-songwriter Jewel. In 1998, Jewel, an avid rider, was at UConn, scheduled to perform at Jorgensen Auditorium. During her brief visit to UConn, she was offered a trail ride on Salem, accompanied by Kathy Pelletier on the mare, UC Sonata. Jewel and Salem became instant friends. Salem was a gracious hostess, carrying the performer through the hidden trails and paths behind UConn's campus. They rode for over two fun hours.

Salem was a mare that had a quiet, sensitive grace. She displayed blissful gratitude when her mud-coated flanks were curried and burrs were gently removed from her tail, one by one. Her eyes would close and her muzzle would quiver as she leaned into the brush.

Years later, Kathy Pelletier gave Salem a richly deserved retirement at her nearby home. There, Salem enjoyed long, lazy days and heaps of adoration from Kathy's daughter, Courtney. The record-breaking World Champion lived to an advanced age. When she left this world, the sweet and beautiful Salem Sentana took many hearts with her.

In The Bridle, 2012

123

The Groom

Before the sunrise, the morning is still
Nostrils billow steam and nickers fill the air
A flake of hay is thrown over the stall door
A scoop of molasses-scented oats in the tub
Wheelbarrow full and wet, tire nearly flat
Leather snaps stubbornly and bits jingle brightly
My hands know where to go
My eyes know what to see
All day into evening I heed these souls
At day's end I fall asleep in a narrow wooden bunk
And I embrace the pre-dawn dark yet again.

~Helen Scanlon 8/28/11

Glimpses into History
"We loved our horses."

Andy Carter is "the guardian of the horse barn." He has been in college employ for many years, and has endeared himself to all those who have come in close contact with him. His cheery disposition, even temper, and kindliness have also enabled him to win hearts of all "his horses."

Each animal is carefully tended and under his supervision, and nothing interferes with the daily routine of these chores. Every horse has a particular spot in Mr. Carter's heart, and his pride of them all is shown by the way he points them out to interested visitors. Andy can doctor minor ailments like a professional, and many times he has stayed up all night to take care of sick horses or a newborn colt. He is a past master in breaking and training horses, and as he understands these animals thoroughly, he never has to employ any but gentle methods, to gain the desired results.

~1937 *Connecticut State College (UConn) Block and Bridle Review*

Horsewoman Supreme

A blonde, graceful woman on a handsome mount accompanied by a beautiful Dalmatian could mean but one thing on the Connecticut campus nowadays. Miss Adelaide Connolly is exercising one of her horses. Now in charge of the riding stables at the University of Connecticut, Miss Connolly has operated her own stable in Pleasant Valley, Willimantic.

Miss Connolly has participated in horse shows throughout the state and has taken part in all but one of the Block and Bridle shows at the University of Connecticut. She took first place in the local saddle horse class in the contest held last May on Sachem Peavine, owned by Dr. Robert Rafferty of Willimantic whose horses she has shown for some time.

Born in Holyoke, Massachusetts, Miss Connolly had a pony when she was small, and she has owned many horses since then. At one time, she worked for J.P. Westcott's stable in Dover, Massachusetts. Her duties at the University consist of handling the riding stable, and instructing horsemanship to students, faculty, and children in the Storrs community. The Block and Bridle Club invited her to become an honorary member last winter.

~1944 *UConn Block and Bridle Review*

This year we welcome back a familiar face to our barns. Bruce Walters, class of 1958 and the Premier Showman that year, is our new horseman. Bruce came here in September from Green Mountain Stock Farm in Vermont. He has had a great deal of experience working with Morgan horses as well as beef cattle. Bruce, and his wife, Carol, raise Irish Setters as a hobby.

~1965 *UConn Block and Bridle Review*

Showmanship Class, 1945

The Block and Bridle Review

Published by the C. S. C. Block and Bridle Club

VOL. VIII.   STORRS, CONN., MAY 7, 1938   Number 1

THE MORGAN HORSE

Legend has it that back in 1795, Justin Morgan, a school teacher at Randolph, accepted a three-year-old gelding and a two-year-old stallion colt as payment for a debt. The gelding has long since been forgotten, but the colt is widely known in horse circles today as the founder of the Morgan breed.

This colt became known by the name of its owner as he grew famous not only for his beauty of conformation, but for his speed in running short distances. Races of about eighty rods were common in those days. The group that convened at the tavern or the village grocery store had almost a sure bet when they put their money on Justin Morgan. His short legs and heavy muscles sent him off with a quick start to a flying finish. Repeated trials proved that he could out-draw, out-walk, out-trot, and out-run all competitors.

In conformation, Justin Morgan excelled in having close jointed, short legs, remarkable muscular development, and wide, clean, hard bone above shapely feet. Though his mane and tail were course, his coat was fine and glossy. Dark, prominent eyes, and large nostrils indicated spirit, with a pleasing disposition. He was a close coupled horse, with an exceedingly strong, broad top, measuring about fourteen hands and weighing nearly nine hundred and fifty pounds. Reports vary from twenty-nine to thirty-two years as the length of his life.

In action, Justin Morgan was "something to write home about". He possessed great speed and style at the walk, and his trot was slow and smooth. His movement has been characterized as proud, bold, and fearless, making him in demand at military reviews where he commanded much praise and attention.

Justin Morgan sired uniformity of type, size, form, temperament, constitution and action. Some of his most noted sons to carry on the breed were the Hawkins Horse, the Fenton Horse, Revenge, Sherman Morgan, Woodbury Morgan, and Bulrush Morgan.

The Morgan breed has contributed so much to other breeds that sometimes the contributions have proven detrimental to the Morgan. To the American Trotter, it gave constitution strength, and staying qualities, while the American Saddle Horse used Morgan blood to obtain finish, spirit, style, beauty, and docility of disposition.

The Morgan Horse Club was organized in 1909. Prior to that Joseph Battell of Middlebury, Vermont, had become interested in and attempted to restore the Morgan Horse, which had been waning in popularity. He compiled the first two volumes of the Morgan Horse Register, now conducted by the Morgan Horse Club. Today horses must show a large percentage of Morgan blood to be eligible for registry.

Instrumental in preserving Morgan type has been the United States Morgan Horse Farm at Bennington, Vermont. Activities at this farm were begun in 1905 in cooperation with the Vermont Experiment Station, an attempt being made to retain all the good qualities of the Morgan, while increasing the size and quality. Early in 1907, Colonel Joseph Battell (mentioned above) presented the Department of Agriculture his farm of 400 acres at Middlebury, to be used in connection with this work. At the head of the stud was placed General Gates 666, great grandsire of Canfield, the stallion now at the Connecticut State College here at Storrs. The Morgans bred by the government at Middlebury have proven very popular, and have been exported to Japan, Brazil, Peru, several Central American Republics, and the West Indies, as well as being sold in fourteen states here in America.

At first the Morgans were primarily road horses, but they have become popular from the saddle standpoint, and are being bred for that today. The modern Morgan is very similiar to the original ones, with some increase in size and quality, and more emphasis on fine, sloping shoulders, well-defined withers, and a long "breedy" neck.

Morgan horses are noted for endurance and adaptability They have been used creditably as roadsters, heavy-harness horses, saddle horses, cavalry horses, and hunters. Today they are being bred especially for saddle use.

The chief stronghold of the Morgan horse today is New England and New York, though there are some breeders in the western states. The Morgans future is promising and will probably continue to increase in distribution and popularity.

※※※※※※※※※※※※※※※※※※※※※※※※

The horse on the cover is the Morgan Stallion, Abbott.

※※※※※※※※※※※※※※※※※※※※※※※※

RIDIN'

There is some that likes the city—
Grass that's carried smooth and green,
Theaytres and stranglin' collars,
Wagons run by gasoline—
But for me it's hawse and saddle
Every day without a change,
And a desert sun a-blazin'
On a hundred miles of range.
Just a-ridin', a-ridin'—
Desert ripplin' in the sun,
Mountains blue along the skyline—
When I'm ridin'.

I don't need no art exhibits
When the sunset does her best,
Paintin' everlastin' glory
On the mountains to the west,
And your opery looks foolish
When the night-bird starts his tune
And the desert's silver mounted
By the touches of the moon.
Just a-ridin', a-ridin'—
Who kin envy kings and czars
When the coyotes down the valley
Are a-singin' to the stars—
If he's ridin'?

When my earthly trail is ended,
And my final bacon curled
And the last great roundup's finished
At the Home Ranch of the world
I don't want no harps nor haloes
Robes nor other dressed up things—
Let me ride the starry ranges
On a pinto hawse with wings.
Just a-ridin', a-ridin'—
Nothin' I'd like so well
As a roundin' up the sinners
That have wandered out of Hell,
And a-ridin'.

                              Badger Clark

Courtesy of the Vermont Horse and Bridle Trail Bulletin

THE TENNESSEE WALKING HORSE

The Tennessee walking Horse was first bred in middle Tennessee one hundred years ago. This horse has four very distinct gaits, a running walk, a flat walk, a sweeping fox trot and a roling canter.

All of these gaits are performed with the rider sitting the saddle perfectly flat and relaxed.

The Walking Horse is strictly a pleasure mount, and has recently been called "The Worlds Greatest Pleasure Horse".

This coming fall we expect to see these horses entered in many of our Eastern Horse Shows.

1938 UConn Block and Bridle Review

THE LITTLE INTERNATIONAL

The exhibition and competition of livestock at shows and fairs has played an important role in upgrading and formulating standards and ideals of the kinds of livestock suited for specific purposes. The show ring has given the livestock breeder a pattern or direction toward which to point his selection of breeding stock. In addition, it has aroused the interest of the general public and keeps the public aware of the place of livestock in the agricultural and national economy.

There is much more to animal husbandry, however, than just the show itself. The show and the ribbon may represent one of the end points or goals but sound selection and breeding, proper feeding, sensible management, attention to details and much training are all prerequisites before the animal enters the ring.

This day is show day. It has been long awaited. This day the student in competition has the opportunity to prove what he knows about fitting and showing livestock. It is, in a sense, an examination of the student on his livestock sense and handling ability. Perhaps even greater than that, it gives him a chance to develop and demonstrate if he has what it takes for the race of life—to struggle to excel, to win fairly and with modesty, and if he loses to do so graciously and congratulate the man that has topped him.

This type of show does more than develop livestock handling ability and know how. It helps build character, personality, responsibility and associations with others. It is a part of general education that every one must learn sooner or later if his way along the path of life is to be fairly smooth and successful.

We are most happy to welcome you to see for yourself the job that these students have done with their livestock. We believe you will see a great show and some good livestock. We believe that you will be happy that you were able to sit and watch the development of young people of purpose and character.

W. A. Cowan,
Head Animal Industries Dept.

UConn Morgan Drill Team, 1994

Showing In-Hand , 1964

UConn Mare Lines

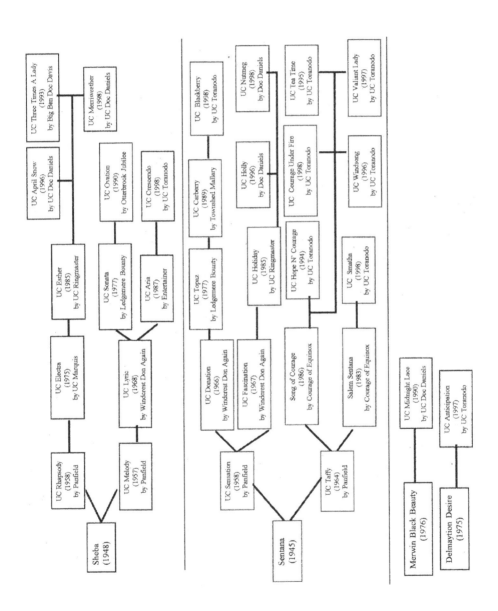

Morgan Horses Bred at
The University of Connecticut

YOB	NAME	SIRE	DAM
1942	MAC ARTHUR	GOLDFIELD	ROMANCE
1944	GOLDEN JOY	GOLDFIELD	JOYOUS
1946	QUADRILLE	NILES	JOYCE
1947	COLT	MENTOR	JOYCE
1948	COLT	MENTOR	JOYCE
1949	CANNONEER	CANFIELD	SCOTCH MELODY
1949	CANNIE	CANFIELD	PHILLIPA
1949	OH BE JOYFUL	CANFIELD	GOLDER JOY
1949	MANNA	MENTOR	DIANA
1949	MEG	CANFIELD	PEGGY
1949	FILLY	PANFIELD	JOYCE
1950	SUNNFIELD	CANFIELD	PEGGY
1951	UC ESTELLITA	STELLAR	PENNSY
1951	UC HI-NOON	MENTOR	QUOTATION
1951	UC KNIGHT	MENTOR	PENNYROYAL
1951	UC PHOENIX	SUREFOOT	MEADOWLARK
1952	UC MENTION	?	?
1952	UC PANELLA	PANFIELD	MABLE MORGAN
1952	UC PANDORA	?	?
1952	FILLY	MENTOR	QUOTATION
1952	FILLY	MENTOR	PENNYROYAL
1952	UC PANYLN	?	?
1953	UC HERMES	MEADE	HERMINA
1953	UC MEBBA	MENTOR	SHEBA
1953	UC PENTOR	MENTOR	PENNSY
1953	UC QUOTOR	MENTOR	QUOTATION
1954	UC CANTOR	MENTOR	CANNIE
1954	UC HERMIT	MENTOR	HERMINA

YOB	NAME	SIRE	DAM
1954	UC PANDRA	PANFIELD	ADLYNDRA
1954	UC PENTORA	MENTOR	PENNSY
1954	UC QUOMEN	MENTOR	QUOTATION
1954	UC SENTORA	MENTOR	SENTANA
1954	UC TORSHA	MENTOR	SHEBA
1955	UC MANEZ	?	?
1955	#105	MENTOR	HERMINA
1955	UC PANQUOTA	PANFIELD	QUOTATION
1955	UC PANTANA	PANFIELD	SENTANA
1955	UC SANDRA	PANFIELD	ADLYNDRA
1955	UC TORIN	?	?
1956	UC SERENADE	PANFIELD	SHEBA
1956	UC STUDENT PRINCE	MENTOR	UC PANELLA
1957	UC COUNTRY BOY	PANFIELD	HERMINA
1957	UC HIGH LIFE	MENTOR	UC PANETTE
1957	UC MAIN EVENT	PANFIELD	UCONN ESTELLITA
1957	UC MELODIE	PANFIELD	SHEBA
1957	MENFIELD	TOPFIELD	QUAKERLADY
1957	UC PACEMAKER	MENTOR	CANNIE
1957	UC PANELLA P	MENTOR	UC PANELLA
1957	UC PENFIELD	PANFIELD	PENNSY
1957	UC SPARKLER	WINDCREST DONFIELD	OPTIC
1957	UC TORADORA	MENTOR	UC PANDORA
1958	UC BOUNCER	MENTOR	UC PANETTE
1958	UC JESTER	MENTOR	UC PANELLA
1958	UC PENSIVE	MENTOR	PENNSY
1958	UC RHAPSODY	PANFIELD	SHEBA
1958	UC SENSATION	PANFIELD	SENTANA
1958	UC TEACHER'S PET	MENTOR	CANNIE
1958	UC WINSOME	MENTOR	WIN-EVE
1958	UC CONQUISTADOR	MENTOR	UC PANDORA
1959	UC CAVALIER	PANFIELD	QUAKERLADY
1959	UC HAPPY TUNE	MENTOR	TUNEFUL
1959	UC LOVELY VISION	WINDCREST DONFIELD	OPTIC

YOB	NAME	SIRE	DAM
1959	UC STRUTTER	PANFIELD	UVM ADDISON MAID
1959	UC TROUBADOUR	PANFIELD	SHEBA
1960	UC CANDY	MENTOR	CANNIE
1960	UC HARMONY	PANFIELD	SHEBA
1960	UC LEADER	MENTOR	SENTANA
1960	UC LYNN	MENTOR	LYNDA
1960	UC SENORITA	PANFIELD	UC SENTORA
1961	UC SENATOR	MENTOR	SENTANA
1961	UC EXHILARATION	THE EXPLORER	UC MELODIE
1961	UC EXPECTATION	THE EXPLORER	CANNIE
1961	UC EXPLORATION	THE EXPLORER	OPTIC
1961	UC EXULTATION	THE EXPLORER	UC SENTORA
1961	UC REVERIE	PANFIELD	SHEBA
1961	UC ROMANCER	MENTOR	UC SERENADE
1962	UC ECSTASY	THE EXPLORER	SENTANA
1962	UC EXCALIBUR	THE EXPLORER	CANNIE
1962	UC EXCELSIOR	THE EXPLORER	UC MELODIE
1962	UC EXPRESSION	THE EXPLORER	UC SERENADE
1962	UC SYMPHONY	PANFIELD	SHEBA
1963	UC FANTASY	PANFIELD	SENTANA
1963	UC LADY	PANFIELD	SENTANA
1963	UC MAESTRO	PANFIELD	QUAKERLADY
1963	UC PROMENADE	PARADE	UC SENSATION
1964	UC BATON	PARADE	CANNIE
1964	UC MAJORETTE	PARADE	UC SENSATION
1964	UC TAFFY	PANFIELD	SENTANA
1964	UC TEMPO	PANFIELD	SHEBA
1965	UC DEACON	PANFIELD	QUAKERLADY
1965	UC EVA	TOWNSHEND VIGALVIN	MONTAIN MEADOW EVE
1965	UC FINALE	PANFIELD	SHEBA

YOB	NAME	SIRE	DAM
1965	UC PRIMA DONA	WINDCREST DON AGAIN	UC RHAPSODY
1966	UC CONCERTINA	WINDCREST DON AGAIN	UC MELODIE
1966	UC DAWN	MENTOR	MOUNTAIN MEADOW EVE
1966	UC DONATION	WINDCREST DON AGAIN	UC SENSATION
1966	UC DONDI	WINDCREST DON AGAIN	UC RHAPSODY
1966	UC HEATHER	WINDCREST DON AGAIN	SHEBA
1967	UC ALLEGRO	WINDCREST DON AGAIN	UC MELODIE
1967	UC ATHENA	WINDCREST DON AGAIN	UC EXPECTATION
1967	UC CALIPH	WINDCREST DON AGAIN	SHEBA
1967	UC FASCINATION	WINDCREST DON AGAIN	UC SENSATION
1967	UC CHARITY	WINDCREST DON AGAIN	QUAKERLADY
1967	UC MARQUIS	WINDCREST DON AGAIN	CANNIE
1967	VISCOUNT	WINDCREST DON AGAIN	MOUNTAIN MEADOW EVE
1968	UC AMBASSADOR	WINDCREST DON AGAIN	CANNIE
1968	UC APOLLO	WINDCREST DON AGAIN	UC EXPECTATION
1968	UC DARK SHADOW	WINDCREST DON AGAIN	UC RHAPSODY
1968	UC FLIRTATION	WINDCREST DON AGAIN	UC SENSATION
1968	UC LYRIC	WINDCREST DON AGAIN	UC MELODIE
1968	UC PLAYBOY	WINDCREST DON AGAIN	UC FANTASY
1968	UC TWILIGHT	WINDCREST DON AGAIN	MOUNTAIN MEADOW EVE

YOB	NAME	SIRE	DAM
1969	UC BALLERINA	WINDCREST DON AGAIN	UC RHAPSODY
1969	UC CALYPSO	WINDCREST DON AGAIN	UC MELODIE
1969	UC COMMOTION	WINDCREST DON AGAIN	UC SENSATION
1969	UC GRANDEE	WINDCREST DON AGAIN	CANNIE
1971	UC CONTESSA	UC MARQUIS	UC RHAPSODY
1971	UC LE BARON	WINDCREST DON AGAIN	CANNIE
1971	UC NEON (unregistered)	WINDCREST DON AGAIN	FOXY ANN
1971	UC REFLECTION	WINDCREST DON AGAIN	UC SENSATION
1971	UC SOLITAIRE	WINDCREST DON AGAIN	UC HARMONY
1971	UC SPICY LASS	UC MARQUIS	UC TAFFY
1971	UC VAGABOND	WINDCREST DON AGAIN	UC MELODIE
1972	UC CRACKERJACK	WINDCREST DON AGAIN	UC TAFFY
1972	UC DUCHESS	WINDCREST DON AGAIN	UC RHAPSODY
1972	UC MINSTREL	UC MARQUIS	UC MELODIE
1972	UC PROPHET	UC MARQUIS	UC EXPECTATION
1972	UC ROYAL FOX	UC MARQUIS	FOXY ANN
1972	UC TARA	WINDCREST DON AGAIN	UC TORSHA
1973	UC BALLADEER	UC MARQUIS	UC MELODIE
1973	UC LEGACY	WINDCREST DON AGAIN	CANNIE
1973	UC NOUGAT	UC MARQUIS	UC TAFFY
1973	UC PREDICTOR	UC MARQUIS	UC EXPECTATION
1973	UC VIXON	UC MARQUIS	FOXY ANN
1974	UC ACROBAT	ORCLAND JOHN DARLING	UC LYRIC

135

YOB	NAME	SIRE	DAM
1974	UC ARCHER	ORCLAND JOHN DARLING	UC DONATION
1974	UC CARILLON	ORCLAND JOHN DARLING	UC MELODIE
1974	UC DESTINY	UC MARQUIS	UC FASCINATION
1974	UC HOPEFUL	ORCLAND JOHN DARLING	UC CHARITY
1974	UC LUCKY KIT	ORCLAND JOHN DARLING	FOXY ANN
1974	UC SENMARA	UC MARQUIS	UC SENSATION
1975	UC CARAMEL	UC MARQUIS	UC TAFFY
1975	UC CASANOVA	UC MARQUIS	UC FLIRTATION
1975	UC DESTINY	UC MARQUIS	UC FASCINATION
1975	UC ELECTRA	UC MARQUIS	UC RHAPSODY
1976	UC CERES	LEDGEMERE BOUNTY	UC CHARITY
1976	UC CORNUCOPIA	LEDGEMERE BOUNTY	UC EXPECTATION
1976	UC FOXGLOVE	LEDGEMERE BOUNTY	FOXY ANN
1976	UC HARVESTOR	LEDGEMERE BOUNTY	UC CHARITY
1976	UC LIBERTY BELLE	UC MARQUIS	UC SENSATION
1976	UC VINTNER	LEDGEMERE BOUNTY	UC LYRIC
1977	UC BON CHER	LEDGEMERE BOUNTY	UC CHARITY
1977	UC CHOCOLADE	UC MARQUIS	UC TAFFY
1977	UC CODQUETTE	LEDGEMERE BOUNTY	UC FLIRTATION
1977	UC ECHO	LEDGEMERE BOUNTY	UC RHAPSODY
1977	UC SONATA	LEDGEMERE BOUNTY	UC LYRIC
1977	UC TIP TOP	LEDGEMERE BOUNTY	UC SENSATION
1977	UC TOPAZ	LEDGEMERE BOUNTY	UC DONATION
1977	UC ZESTY	LEDGEMERE BOUNTY	UC SPICY LASS
1978	UC ORION	LEDGEMERE BOUNTY	UC EXPECTATION
1978	UC RINGMASTER	WASEEKA'S SHOWTIME	UC LYRIC
1978	UC SPORTSMAN	LEDGEMERE BOUNTY	UC SENSATION
1978	UC SUNDOWNER	LEDGEMERE BOUNTY	UC FASCINATION
1979	UC CHARISMA	CORISHAM	UC CHARITY

YOB	NAME	SIRE	DAM
1979	UC CINNAMON	UVM VIKING	UC SPICY LASS
1979	UC IRISH MIST	BENNFIELD'S ACE	UC RHAPSODY
1979	UC LEPRECHAUN	UVM VIKING	UC CONCERTINA
1979	UC MELODEON	GALLANT LEE	UC LYRIC
1979	UC PEPPERMINT	UVM VIKING	UC TAFFY
1979	UC RHYTHMAIRE	SERENITY MARCH TIME	UC FASCINATION
1979	UC STANZA	UVM VIKING	UC HARMONY
1980	UC ACE HIGH	BENNFIELD'S ACE	UC LYRIC
1980	UC COVER GIRL	UVM TROPHY	MERWIN BLACK BEAUTY
1980	UC DANEGELD	UVM VIKING	UC DONATION
1980	UC DOUBLOON	DELMAYTION GLIDER	DELMAYTION EMERALD
1980	UC FIRST EDITION	UVM VIKING	DELMAYTION DESIRE
1980	UC VALHALLA	UVM VIKING	UC CHARITY
1981	UC ADVENTURER	UC RINGMASTER	UC SENMARA
1981	UC CALLIOPE	WASEEKA'S SHOWTIME	UC SONATA
1981	UC ESQUIRE	UC RINGMASTER	UC BON CHER
1981	UC HIGH ROLLER	CORISHAM	UC ELECTRA
1981	UC JAZZ MAN	UC RINGMASTER	UC CONCERTINA
1981	UC KISMET	UC RINGMASTER	UC FASCINATION
1981	UC KIWI	UC RINGMASTER	MERWIN BLACK BEAUTY
1982	UC MERLIN	UC RINGMASTER	UC FASCINATION
1982	UC ORBITOR	UC RINGMASTER	UC DONATION
1982	UC SUNDANCE	UC RINGMASTER	MERWIN BLACK BEAUTY
1982	UC TOWN CRIER	UC RINGMASTER	DELMAYTION DESIRE
1982	UC WANDERER	UC RINGMASTER	UC SONATA
1983	UC LANCELOT	UC RINGMASTER	UC CONCERTINA
1983	UC MR SOLO	UC RINGMASTER	UC DONATION
1983	MR PHOEBE	UC RINGMASTER	MERWIN BLACK BEAUTY

YOB	NAME	SIRE	DAM
1983	UC RINGLEADER	WASEEKA'S SHOWTIME	UC LYRIC
1983	UC TOP BRASS	UC RINGMASTER	UC FASCINATION
1984	UC CENTERFOLD	UC RINGMASTER	MERWIN BLACK BEAUTY
1984	UC RIANNA	UC RINGMASTER	UC IRISH MIST
1984	UC SERENDIPITY	UC RINGMASTER	DELMAYTION DESIRE
1984	UC STAR FIRE	UC RINGMASTER	UC TOPAZ
1985	UC DAYBREAK	UC RINGMASTER	DELMAYTION DESIRE
1985	UC ESTHER	UC RINGMASTER	UC ELECTRA
1985	UC HOLIDAY	UC RINGMASTER	UC FASCINATION
1985	UC WILDE MARK (ET)	UC RINGMASTER	UC FASCINATION
1987	UC ARIA	ENTERTAINER	UC LYRIC
1987	UC DOC DANIELS	UVM ELITE	UC TOPAZ
1987	UC TOP GUN	MAD RIVER SAILOR	UC FASCINATION
1988	UC DESIREE	CHANTWOOD COMMAND	DELMAYTION DESIRE
1988	UC ENTERTAINE ME	ENTERTAINER	MERWIN BLACK BEAUTY
1988	UC JUSTA FLIRT	CHANTWOOD COMMAND	UC FLIRTATION
1988	UC ROYAL LADY	HI-VALE ROYAL MAN	UC SONATA
1988	UC ROYAL MAN	HI-VALE ROYAL MAN	UC ELECTRA
1988	UC SHOW BIZ	WASEEKA'S SHOWTIME	UC LYRIC
1988	UC TOP HAT	UC RINGMASTER	UC FASCINATION
1989	UC ARISTOCRAT	UVM ELITE	UC CONCERTINA
1989	UC CARBERRY	TOWNSHEND MELARRY	UC TOPAZ
1989	UC ENCOURAGER	COURAGE OF EQUINOX	UC LYRIC
1989	UC FLIRTING FOOL	HI-VALE ROYAL MAN	UC FLIRTATION
1989	UC ONYX	UC RINGMASTER	MERWIN BLACK BEAUTY
1989	UC TOP THIS	UC RINGMASTER	UC FASCINATION
1989	UC TRAVELER	APPLEVALE VOYAGER	UC CARILLON

YOB	NAME	SIRE	DAM
1990	UC CITY LIGHTS	HERALD SQUARE	UC ELECTRA
1990	UC LAST TANGO	UC WILDE MARK	DELMAYTION DESIRE
1990	UC MIDNIGHT LACE	UC DOC DANIELS	MERWIN BLACK BEAUTY
1990	UC OVATION	OTTER BROOK JUBILEE	UC SONATA
1990	UC ROYAL DUTCHESS	HI-VALE ROYAL MAN	UC FLIRTATION
1990	UC SQUIRE	UC DOC DANIELS	UC CONCERTINA
1990	UC TORONADO	TEDWIN TAUREAN	UC FASCINATION
1991	UC DOC'S IMAGE	UC DOC DANIELS	MERWIN BLACK BEAUTY
1991	UC FANCY BIZNESS	UC SHOW BIZ	UC FASCINATION
1991	UC HAMMERTIME	TRIJAS MR PEPPERLECT	SALEM SENTANA
1991	UC HARRY H	HERALD SQUARE	UC CONCERTINA
1992	UC ARTHUR L	UC SHOW BIZ	DELMAYTION DESIRE
1992	UC BIZ E FLIRTING	UC SHOW BIZ	UC FLIRTATION
1992	UC BUCKINGHAM	UC DOC DANIELS	MERWIN BLACK BEAUTY
1992	UC KATYDID	UC DOC DANIELS	KATY ELDER
1992	UC SHOW GIRL	UC SHOW BIZ	UC FASCINATION
1992	UC SONGMASTER	SORENTO	UC SONATA
1992	UC SPRING BREAK	UC SHOW BIZ	CLF'S BUTTER CUP
1993	UC BROADWAY SHOW	UC SHOW BIZ	CLF'S BUTTER CUP
1993	UC CENTER STAGE	SORENTO	UC CENTERFOLD
1993	UC THREE TIMES A LADY	BIG BEN DOC DAVIS	UC ESTHER
1994	UC ARIEL	QUAL-LITY CONTROL	UC ARIA
1994	UC CELEBRITY	UC SHOW BIZ	DELMAYTION DESIRE
1994	UC CONCERTO	UC TORONADO	UC SONATA
1994	UC HOPE AND COURAGE	UC TORONADO	SONG OF COURAGE

139

YOB	NAME	SIRE	DAM
1994	UC NIGHT FLIGHT	SORENTO	UC CENTERFOLD
1995	UC BLACK TIE AFFAIR	UC TORONADO	UC CENTERFOLD
1995	UC CURTIS	UC SHOW BIZ	DELMAYTION DESIRE
1995	UC MOONSHADOW	UC TORONADO	UC CARBERRY
1995	UC NAVIGATOR	UC DOC DANIELS	CBF'S MANDY
1995	UC TEE TIME	UC TORONADO	SONG OF COURAGE
1996	UC APRIL SNOW	UC DOC DANIELS	UC ESTHER
1996	UC BLACK RAZBERRY	UC TORONADO	UC CARBERRY
1996	UC HOLLY	UC DOC DANIELS	UC HOLIDAY
1996	UC OLYMPIC STAR	UC DOC DANIELS	UC ARIA
1996	UC ROGUE	UC DOC DANIELS	CBF'S MANDY
1996	UC WARLOCK	UC TORONADO	SALEM SENTANA
1996	UC WINDSONG	UC TORONADO	SONG OF COURAGE
1997	UC ANTICIPATION	UC TORONADO	DELMAYTION DESIRE
1997	UC LEONARDO	UC TORONADO	UC MIDNIGHT LACE
1997	UC TRIUMPH	UC DOC DANIELS	UC OVATION
1997	UC VALIENT LADY	UC TORONADO	SONG OF COURAGE
1997	UC VERTIGO	UC DOC DANIELS	UVM VERITY
1998	UC SAMANTHA	UC TORONADO	SALEM SENTANA
1998	UC MERRIWEATHER	UC DOC DANIELS	UC ESTHER
1998	UC BLACKBERRY	UC TORONADO	UC CARBERRY
1998	UC DOC TARI	UC DOC DANIELS	UVM VERITY
1998	UC BOLERO	UC TORONADO	UC MIDNIGHT LACE
1998	UC CRESCENDO	UC TORONADO	UC ARIA
1998	UC NUTMEG	UC DOC DANIELS	UC HOLIDAY
1998	UC COURAGE UNDER FIRE	UC TORONADO	SONG OF COURAGE

YOB	NAME	SIRE	DAM
1999	UC NIGHTRIDER	HILLFIELD NIGHT RIDER	UC HOPE AND COURAGE
1999	UC TRIUMPH	UC DOC DANIELS	UC SONATA
1999	UC MIDNIGHT MISCHEIF	UC TORONADO	UC MIDNIGHT LACE
1999	UC IRISH RHAPSODY	UC TORONADO	UC ESTHER
1999	UC FAITH	UC TORONADO	UVM VERITY
1999	UC MAYBERRY	UC TORONADO	UC CARBERRY
1999	UC FASCINATIN RHYTHM	UC DOC DANIELS	UC HOLIDAY
1999	UC BRAVE HEART	UC TORONADO	SONG OF COURAGE
2000	UC BRAVO	UC TORONADO	UC OVATION
2000	UC EXCALIBUR	UC DOC DANIELS	SALEM SENTANA
2000	UC MR T'S DESTINY	UC TORONADO	UC ARIA
2000	UC CENTURY	UC TORONADO	UVM VERITY
2000	UC HUCKLEBERRY	UC DOC DANIELS	UC CARBERRY
2000	UC MISTY	UC DOC DANIELS	SONG OF COURAGE
2000	UC MINUET	UVM SPRINGFIELD	UC SONATA
2000	UC CINNAMON	UVM SPRINGFIELD	UC HOLIDAY
2001	UC CADBERRY	UC DOC DANIELS	UC CARBERRY
2001	UC HIGH HOPES	UC DOC DANIELS	UC HOPE AND COURAGE
2001	UC JACK DANIELS	UC DOC DANIELS	UC ESTHER
2001	UC MIDNIGHT SPECIAL	UC TORONADO	UC MIDNIGHT LACE
2001	UC SPRING LEGEND	UVM SPRINGFIELD	UC HOLIDAY
2002	UC VIRTUE	UC DOC DANIELS	UVM VERITY
2002	UC ARIES	UC DOC DANIELS	UC ARIA
2002	UC FREEDOM	UC RINGMASTER	UC HOPE AND COURAGE
2002	UC TEE ROSE	UC RINGMASTER	UC TEE TIME
2002	UC NIGHTSTAR	UC RINGMASTER	UC MIDNIGHT LACE
2003	UC PERFECT STRIDE	UC RINGMASTER	SALEM SENTANA

YOB	NAME	SIRE	DAM
2003	UC BELLA DONNA	UC RINGMASTER	UC HOPE AND COURAGE
2003	UC HOLIDAY PRIDE	UC DOC DANIELS	UC HOLIDAY
2004	UC APPLAUSE	UC DOC DANIELS	UC OVATION
2004	UC DOMINATION	UC DOC DANIELS	UC ARIA
2004	UC LUCKY CHARM	UC DOC DANIELS	UC IRISH RHAPSODY
2005	UC CONTENDER	UC RINGMASTER	UC COURAGE UNDER FIRE
2005	UC MASTER STATESMAN	UC RINGMASTER	STATESMAN'S ANGELS WHISPER
2005	UC DIAMONDS DEVOTION	UC RINGMASTER	UC FAITH
2005	UC MISTY MAY	UC DOC DANIELS	LJB STARLIGHT EXPRESS
2005	UC CELEBRATION	UC DOC DANIELS	UC HOLIDAY
2006	UC SCARLET AFFAIR	UC RINGMASTER	UC COURAGE UNDER FIRE
2006	UC LYRE	UC DOC DANIELS	UC ARIA
2006	UC EMMA	UC DOC DANIELS	UC OVATION
2006	UC VALENTINO	UC RINGMASTER	UC FAITH
2007	UC DOC SANCHEZ	UC DOC DANIELS	UC TEE TIME
2007	UC VEGAS	UC DOC DANIELS	CHINA BAYLES
2007	UC MERCEDES	UC RINGMASTER	UC FAITH
2007	UC CELTIC ROSE	UC DOC DANIELS	UC IRISH RHAPSODY
2008	UC FIREFLY	UC DOC DANIELS	UC COURAGE UNDER FIRE
2008	UC SERENITY	UC RINGMASTER	UC FAITH
2009	UC MASTERMIND	UC RINGMASTER	UC FAITH
2009	UC STAR ABOVE	UC DOC DANIELS	CABOT TOP ATTRACTION

YOB	NAME	SIRE	DAM
2009	UC TEE PARTY	UC DOC DANIELS	UC TEE TIME
2010	UC LIBERTY	UC DOMINATION	UC TEE ROSE
2010	UC DAN THE MAN	UC DOC DANIELS	STATESMANS ANGELS WHISPER
2011	UC MISCHIEF MANAGED	UC DOMINATION	UC COURAGE UNDER FIRE
2011	UC HOLIDAY ROSE	ROSEVALE LEGGO	UC HOLIDAY PRIDE

Acknowledgements

…You gave this book its true heart…

Thank you.

So many people motivated this writer to put the story of the amazing Morgan horses of the University of Connecticut in print. Your stories, research leads, photos, support, encouragement, friendship, and unwavering willingness to help, made this book possible.

To the faculty and staff of the University of Connecticut College of Agriculture and Natural Resources Department of Animal Science: Dr. Al Cowan, Dr. Steven Zinn, Dr. Nathan Hale, John Bennett, Jr., Kathy Pelletier, Jim and Peg Dinger, Janice Callahan, Jennifer Simoniello, and Vanessa Licowski: so much knowledge, expertise, support and firsthand experiences; some of you touched these magnificent horses. Thank you for sharing the wealth with me.

To the following individuals and organizations for your memories, archives, articles, stories, advice, leads and support:
The American Morgan Horse Association (much appreciation to Chris Koliander), The National Museum of the Morgan Horse (many thanks to Amber Broderick), The Dodd Center for Research, Megan Brauch, Arlis Bobb, Cheryl Orcutt, Courtnay Lawrence, Julie Biron, Jaclyn Gagnon, Kristen Buch, Kari Ameer, Megan Thompson, Sarah Brander, Jade Lussier, Mary O'Donovan, Anne Wiktor, Christine Gelineau, Barbara Kristoff, Shirley Glenney, Sandra Bushmich, Aurora Milvae, Bob and Patti Brooks, Peggy Alderman, Esther Noiles, Nancy Tomastik, Lloyd Crawford, Mary Goss, Dr. David Rossi, Dr. Donald Balch, The University of Vermont Morgan Horse Farm (Steve Davis and Marin Melchior), Laura Albrecht, Linda Roto, Pat Forst, Kayleigh Meyer, Caitlin Lewis, Jackie Ross, Liz Goldmann, Deb Field, Timothy Budris, Liz Hocking, Cynthia Wickless, Dorothy Ours, Lynn Babbitt, Arthur Perry, Jr., Victoria Surr, John and Georgia Denman, Elizabeth McGee, Jenn Lazzaro, Kara Famularo, Jackie Ross, Lillian Smith, Jennifer Backs, Ami Tuckerman, Pamela Marsh, Elisabeth Prouty-Gilbride, Suzy Lucine, Kelsey McMullen, Stacey Stearns, Carolyn Stearns, Colleen Goyette, Kim Lindell, Sara Morrison, Theresa Blatt, Nina

144

Quinn, Sarah Bothell, Roxanne Pandolfi and Heather Lake.

Thank you to the many who sent e-mails or "Facebooked" me and told me they rode or owned a UConn-bred Morgan horse, or to share information or leads. I appreciate your input. It validated just how loved and revered these horses are.

To everyone who has supported Sound the Bugle Studio Equine Art and Pet Portraits, I thank you from the bottom of my heart. I love that you love what I do.

To the horses of my life: Your lessons never left me; I can see your faces clear as yesterday. Each one, unique and beautiful, you taught me about trust, friendship and gratitude. Let go, and ride.

To Marguerite Henry and Wesley Dennis: Thanks for lighting a creative fire so many years ago.

To my cats, Skeeter, Ghee, Nim Nim, Big Boy, and Mousekowitz: Thanks for being a calm, loving and peaceful presence in my home, and for inspiring my art and literary endeavors. To all of the cats that have honored me with their vibrant energies and unique personalities over the years: I thank you for comforting the child and loving the adult. You are the bright stars in my evening sky.

To the University of Connecticut Morgan Horses, past, present and future: Thank you for inspiring me to finally pursue my lifelong dream of being a published author. It is an honor to transcribe your history; may you always be remembered.

To UC Ringmaster: Thank you for telling me to paint your portrait and to write your story. You made me realize that I should take that "big step that thrilled me and terrified me at the same time." Somehow, you knew I would do it.

To my incredible friends: Thank you for simply being there and freely offering support, french fries, a listening ear, pizza, advice, sushi, smiles, hugs, chocolate, inspiration, comfort, pickles, chick flicks, ice cream, fun and laughter… and for not telling me I was crazy to write a book. Also, thank you for knowing exactly when to call or e-mail to nudge me out of the dreaded "writer's block." You guys know me so well, how lucky can one person be?

Much, much love. Thanks for coming along for the ride and for keeping me centered.

To my wonderful family: I could hear your kind words and see your smiling faces as I wrote. Thanks for checking in on me and cheering me on all the way. I am blessed, lots of love to all of you.

To my editor, the brilliant and amazing Nancy King—I chose you for a reason. It's only because you are the best! I am proud to call you my friend.

To my husband, Steve: Thank you for designing a beautiful book and for making my dream a reality. Also, thank you for being my best friend. You are the treasure I hold dear in my heart—my love for you could fill many infinite Universes.

Thank you, all.

~Helen Scanlon, 7/1/2013

Two Foals, 2012

About the Author

Helen Scanlon was born in Connecticut with the horse-crazy gene firmly intact. At age four, she saw her first horse and she clearly remembers tears of awe filling her eyes—as if something had clicked into place. From that moment on, she was obsessed with everything equine. Every time a pencil or pen was nestled in her fingers, a horse would appear on the paper, even if that paper was in her brother's favorite books. Her parents quickly learned to buy lots of drawing pads for the young artist.

Helen spent hours in her room drawing and studying horses from books and magazines. Her idol was Wesley Dennis, the artist who illustrated the horse stories of Marguerite Henry. She was amazed at his ability to capture the spirit of the equine and the way he could make them live and breathe on the pages. Inspired by his style, young Helen drew the many horses that galloped in the fields of her imagination.

At age 13, she had a ballpoint pen sketch published in an Arabian horse journal, and at age 14, she won The Hartford Courant Scholastic Art Award for her pencil sketch of an Arabian stallion. In college, she garnered excellent reviews in local newspapers and received mention in Connecticut magazine for her artwork in the multi-artist exhibit "Les Fleurs Du Mal" at the An Coreian Gallery.

Her time at the University of Connecticut offered many adventures: she was a groom for a large dressage facility, a bass player in a garage-punk band, and a DJ at the University's radio station. She drove a rusty pick-up truck and could usually be seen tearing through campus on her mountain bike rushing to get to class.

When she received her BA in Art History and Sociology from UConn, she put her paintbrushes and pencils away for nearly a decade. She often thought about them and the horses that used to dance in her drawing pads.

The cries of the pencils and paintbrushes won out, and in 2002, she began to paint and draw her beloved horses as if she had never stopped.

In 2003, she accepted her first commission and founded Sound the Bugle Studio in her Hampton, Connecticut home.

Helen is now internationally known, with her work featured in private collections in the USA, Canada and the UK. She has been featured in Polo Players' Edition magazine and she was a longtime member of the internationally acclaimed Equine Art Guild (now defunct).

My Horse, My Heart: The Morgan Horses of the University of Connecticut is her first book.

Official website: www.soundthebuglestudio.com
E-mail Helen: soundthebuglestudio@charter.net

"Leave your troubles on the ground, swing a leg over, let it go---and just ride."

~The Morgan Horse

Sources

Websites

http://www.morganhorse.com/about_the_morgan/
> Informational webpage from the American Morgan Horse Association website.

http://www.morganmuseum.org
> National Museum of the Morgan Horse.

http://www.morganmuseum.org/html/figure.html
> The Life and Times of Figure.

http://www.morganmuseum.org/html/justinmorgan.html
> Justin Morgan the Man.

http://www.morganmile.com/
> Information on the Morgan Mile in Vermont.

http://www.welcomeranch.com/showtime.html
> Great webpage dedicated to the immortal stallion, Waseeka's Showtime.

http://animalscience.uconn.edu/clubs/drill_team/MeetMorgans.htm
> Meet the UConn Drill Team Morgans!

http://www.creamridgemorgans.com/map/VermontTrip.htm
> Great webpage about a Vermont trip to the historically significant places of Morgan horse interest, complete with wonderful photographs.

http://www.foundationmorganhorse.com/
> Informational webpage on foundation Morgan horses.

http://www.morganhorse.com/registry/registry_history/
>History of the Morgan horse registry from the American Morgan Horse Association.

http://www.ctmorgans.org/
>The Connecticut Morgan Horse Association.

http://www.freedomrider.com/fred/rianna.html
>Website about UC Rianna.

http://www.frogmusic.com/test/farm-history.html
>Fun and informational page about Sleipnir Farm.

http://sleipnirmorganhorsefarm.wordpress.com/2011/03/02/u-c-cinnamon/
>All about Sleipnir Farm's beloved mare, UC Cinnamon.

http://www.thesportmorgan.org/flyhawk.htm
>Information on Flyhawk and his legacy.

http://oldmorgans.blogspot.com/
>Great blog on historically significant Morgan horses, with photos.

http://www.virtualvermont.com/history/jmorgan.html
>Website on the history of the Morgan horse.

http://www.uvm.edu/morgan/
>Website for the University of Vermont Morgan Horse Farm, formerly the United States Government Horse Farm.

http://animalscience.uconn.edu/ansci/handbook/labs.htm
>Website on the UConn Animal Science Department.

http://animalscience.uconn.edu/clubs/drill_team/DrillTeamFrameset.htm
>Website on the incredible UConn Morgan Drill Team.

http://www.nysmhs.org/history/wc/index.html
>I love this website. Many pages dedicated to Wind-Crest Farm and the celebrated stallion, Upwey Ben Don.

http://www.cag.uconn.edu/ansci/ansci/equine/
UConnMorganHorseShowTeam.php
 All about the awesome UConn Morgan Horse Show team.

http://www.allbreedpedigree.com
 This website is chock full of information on pedigrees.

Books, Magazines and Documents

Mellin, Jeanne. *The Morgan Horse*. Brattleboro: Steven Greene Press, 1961.
 Book.

Assorted documents from the University of Connecticut College of Agriculture and Natural Resources Department of Animal Science: UConn Morgan Horse registry; a scan of a 1917 Breeders' Gazette article on Dragon, Jr.; a summary of the UConn Horse Program; a scan of an article by Therese Karmel for The Chronicle, Willimantic, CT: "This Morgan a baron that robs your heart"; and a scan of an article from an unknown and undated source, written by Cynthia Weber, "Dr. Al Cowan: A Lasting Influence At UConn & For The Morgan Breed."

Cowan, Dr. W.A., *The Impact and Importance of Morgan Horses from The US Government Horse on Cooperating Land Grant Universities*, Transcript of Panel Discussion University of Connecticut, Storrs, CT. Februrary, 1997. (This important document was generously contributed by Dr. Nathan Hale)

University of Connecticut Block and Bridle programs cited: Year, article, author info (when available) page number(s). (Programs generously contributed by the University of Connecticut College of Agriculture and Natural Resources Department of Animal Science):
 1936, "The Morgan Stallion, Abbott." Page 9.
 1937, "Dragon, Jr." inside front cover.
 1937, "Horse Barn." Page 7.
 1938, "The Morgan Horse." Page 1.
 1942, "Canfield." Page 6.
 1943, "The University of Connecticut Morgans." Page 5.
 1943, "The Morgan Barn." Page 6.
 1944, "Annual Block and Bridle Horse Show." Page 4.
 1944, "A Horsewoman Supreme." Page 4.

1948, "Tack-Room Talk." Pages 5 and 8.

1949, "Down the Stable Aisle" by Katherine Sharpe. Page 3.

1951, "Four New Mares." Page 4.

1951, "Our Cover Boy (Mentor)." Page 1.

1957, "Horse Barn Progress," by Prof. John Kays. Page 27.

1958, "Horse Barn News," by Ann Kramer. Page 16.

1958, "UConn Results at the National Morgan Horse Show," by Richard Montali. Page 16.

1959, "Horse Happenings." Page 16.

1959, "A Tribute (to Prof. Harry Garrigus)," by Mr. Maurice Lockwood, '21. Page 2.

1960, "News of the Livestock." Page 17.

1961, "News of the Livestock." Page 13.

1962, "Horse Whinnies." Page 12.

1962, "Stallion Memories," by Howard Raven, '33. Page 8.

1963, "Equine Exclamations." Page 18.

1965, "Tackroom Talk." Page 21.

1966, "Tackroom Talk." Pages 18 and 19.

1968, "Equine Escapades." Page 19.

1969, "Prof. Harry L. Garrigus." Page 9.

1970, "Horse Horoscopes." Pages 10 and 11.

1971, "Equine Exclamations." Page 12.

1976, "Equine Happenings." Page 29.

1978, "A Legend: UC Prima Dona." Inside Front Cover.

1982, "UConn Victorious at FAVRAH," by Bruce Shulthess. Page 14.

1983, "UConn Morgans Shine." Page 35.

1986, "Horse Barn," by Linda Kata. Page 40.

1989, "Horse Barn Happenings," by John Bennett, Jr. Page 25.

1989, "Horse Practicum," by Megan Chapman. Page 25.

1990, "Equine Happenings" by John Bennett, Jr. and Kathy Pelletier. Pages 26 and 28.

Rebecca Stygar, "Equine Program Far More Than Just Horsing Around" *UConn Advance* May, 2001: 1-2.

Nita Lelyveld, "Descendants of Cavalry Horses Thrive at UConn" *The Hour-Norwalk, CT* June 8, 1991: 11.

Dr. WA Cowan, "The University of Connecticut Morgan Broodmares Past and Present," *Who's Who in New England Morgandom* (NEMHA). 1987: 7-10.

Lori Gershun. "Weybridge Revisited," *Morgan Horse Magazine* August 2010: 36-47.

Leo Beckley, "Panfield: One of the last of the Old-Timers" *Morgan Horse Magazine* October, 1974: 29.

Debbie Huntley, "University of Connecticut News" *Morgan Horse Magazine* October 1974: 29.

Bill Crawford, "I Lost a Good Friend" *Morgan Horse Magazine* Feb. 1978: 40. "Sentana Goes to College" *Morgan Horse Magazine* Nov. 1952: 20.

Phyliss Taylor ,"High Banner Half-Morgan Jumper" *Morgan Horse Magazine* Feb. 1925: 31.

William Glenney. "Mentor 8627: 23 Years Old" *Morgan Horse Magazine* March 1962: 47.

Maj. Gen. P.C. Tsui, "Report on Arrival of Morgans in China," *Morgan Horse Magazine* Feb. 1948: 42.

Mabel Owen, "Great Broodmare Sires from Justin Morgan to the Present" *Morgan Horse Magazine* Sept. 1970: 11.

Mabel Owen, "Reflections on a Vintage Year" *Morgan Horse Magazine* March 1971: 26.

Personal Communications

I did my best to record and to compile all communications with the kind and generous people who contributed information that was used in *My Horse, My Heart*. Some dates are approximate. Many additional alumni, students, riders and owners e-mailed me to let me know that their lives were touched by UConn-bred Morgans, and I appreciate everyone who took the time to write to me.

Dr. WA Cowan, three phone conversations, 2007.
John Bennett, Jr. and Kathy Pelletier, in-person interview and book proposal meeting, August 26, 2010.
Megan Brauch, in-person interviews and e-mails, 2010-2012

Arlis Bobb, in-person interview, Dec. 2010.

Amber Broderick, e-mails, 2010-2012.

Cheryl Orcutt, phone interview, Dec. 12, 2010. We spent over three hours talking about her life with UC Ringmaster.

Jaclyn Gagnon, phone interview, Jan. 29, 2011.

Kristen Buch, phone interview, Feb. 6, 2011.

Julie Biron, phone interview, Feb. 6, 2011.

Sarah Brander, phone interview, Feb. 16, 2011.

Jenn Lazzaro, e-mail, March 5, 2011.

Kara Famularo, e-mail, March 24, 2011.

Lillian Smith, e-mail, March 25, 2011.

Ami Tuckerman, e-mail, March 18, 2011.

Janice Callahan, phone interviews, Feb. 21 and March 24, 2011.

Mary O'Donovan, e-mail and phone interviews, March 6, 8 and 15, 2011. Mary also sent me some lovely photos of UC Doc Daniels.

Anne Wiktor, phone interview and e-mail, March 8, 2011.

Christine Gelineau, phone interview and e-mail, March 18 and 29, 2011.

Barbara Kristoff, phone interview and e-mail, March 2 and April 5, 2011.

Georgia Denham, e-mail, March 30, 2011.

Victoria Surr, e-mail, April 19, 2011.

John Bennett, Jr., in-person interviews, May 3, June 15, June 20, 2011.

Arthur Perry, Jr., e-mail, May 13, 2011.

Kathy Pelletier, in-person interview and e-mails, January 27, 2010 and May 3, 2011.

Dr. Nathan Hale, phone interview and e-mails, May 31 and June 22, 2011.

Kari Ameer, in-person interview, June 6, 2011. I met UC Sonata on this hot June day.

Patti and Bob Brooks, phone interview, June 25, 2011.

Dr. Sandra Bushmich and Aurora Milvae, phone interview, July 1, 2011.

Lynn Babbitt, e-mail, July 15, 2011.

Peggy Alderman, phone interview and e-mails, April 10, 2011 and July 12, 2011.

Dr. Esther Noiles, phone interview, July 8, 2011.

Christina Koliander, e-mails, August 23, 2011.

Nancy Tomastik, in-person interview, Sept. 14, 2011. Nancy also shared her photo albums and scrapbooks.

Shirley Glenney, phone interview, Dec. 2011.

Lloyd Crawford and Dr. David Rossi, phone interview, Dec. 2011.

Timothy Budris, Facebook message, Dec. 2011.

Maren Melchior, e-mails, Dec. 12, 2011.

Dr. Donald Balch, phone interview, Dec. 20, 2011. It was an incredible honor to talk with the original Director of the UVM Morgan Horse Farm.

Deborah Cowles Lussier, Facebook message, 2011.

Jade Lussier, e-mail, Dec. 8, 2011.

Laura Albrecht, phone interview, Dec. 28, 2011.

Theresa Blatt, phone interview, Dec. 2011.

Pat Forst, e-mail, Dec. 12, 2011.

Linda Roto, phone interview, Jan. 6, 2012.

Dr. James and Peg Dinger, in-person interview, Jan. 15, 2012.

Pamela Marsh, e-mail, March 5, 2012.

Liz Goldmann, e-mail, April 15, 2012.

Megan Thompson, Facebook messages and in-person interviews, 2011 and 2012.

Liz Hocking, blog comments, 2011 and 2012.

Courtnay Lawrence, Facebook messages and e-mails, 2011 and 2012.

Kayleigh Meyer, e-mail, June 17, 2012.

Caitlin Lewis, e-mail, June 19, 2012.

ILLUSTRATION CREDITS

i.   University of Connecticut College of Agriculture and Natural Resources Department of Animal Science collection. Used by permission.

viii.   ©2012 Helen Scanlon

1.   ©2012 Helen Scanlon

10.   University of Connecticut College of Agriculture and Natural Resources Department of Animal Science collection. Used by permission.

11.   photo by Helen Scanlon

15.   radiographs by Heather Beach, DVM. Arlis Bobb collection. Used by permission.

19.   Photo by Arlis Bobb. Used by permission.

22.   ©2012 Helen Scanlon

24.   The National Museum of the Morgan Horse collection. Used by permission.

27.   University of Connecticut College of Agriculture and Natural Resources Department of Animal Science collection. Used by permission.

28.   ©2012 Helen Scanlon

29.   University of Connecticut College of Agriculture and Natural Resources Department of Animal Science collection. Used by permission.

31.   The National Museum of the Morgan Horse collection. Used by permission.

33.   Quality Stables/Jackie Ross collection. Used by permission.

36.   The National Museum of the Morgan Horse collection. Used by permission.

39.   ©2012 Helen Scanlon

41.   University of Connecticut College of Agriculture and Natural Resources Department of Animal Science collection. Used by permission.

43.   ©2012 Helen Scanlon

45.   ©2012 Helen Scanlon

47.   ©2012 Helen Scanlon

50. University of Connecticut College of Agriculture and Natural Resources Department of Animal Science collection. Used by permission.

59. photo by Helen Scanlon

60. ©2012 Helen Scanlon

62. University of Connecticut College of Agriculture and Natural Resources Department of Animal Science collection. Used by permission.

63. Photo by Mary Goss. Used by permission.

65. University of Connecticut College of Agriculture and Natural Resources Department of Animal Science collection. Used by permission.

67. University of Connecticut College of Agriculture and Natural Resources Department of Animal Science collection. Used by permission.

69. ©2012 Helen Scanlon

75. ©2012 Helen Scanlon

77. University of Connecticut College of Agriculture and Natural Resources Department of Animal Science collection. Used by permission.

85. ©2012 Helen Scanlon

93. ©2012 Helen Scanlon

95. ©2012 Helen Scanlon

100. photo by Helen Scanlon

104. University of Connecticut College of Agriculture and Natural Resources Department of Animal Science collection. Used by permission.

105. University of Connecticut College of Agriculture and Natural Resources Department of Animal Science collection. Used by permission.

106. ©2012 Helen Scanlon

111. photo by Alan Buch. Used by permission.

119. Jaclyn Gagnon collection. Used by permission.

123. ©2012 Helen Scanlon

124. ©2012 Helen Scanlon

126. University of Connecticut College of Agriculture and Natural Resources Department of Animal Science collection. Used by permission.

127. University of Connecticut College of Agriculture and Natural Resources Department of Animal Science collection. Used by permission.

128. University of Connecticut College of Agriculture and Natural Resources Department of Animal Science collection. Used by permission.

129. *Top*: University of Connecticut College of Agriculture and Natural Resources Department of Animal Science collection. Courtesy of Kathy Pelletier. Used by permission.
Bottom: University of Connecticut College of Agriculture and Natural Resources Department of Animal Science collection. Used by permission.

130. University of Connecticut College of Agriculture and Natural Resources Department of Animal Science collection. Used by permission. Provided by Dr. James Dinger.

131. University of Connecticut College of Agriculture and Natural Resources Department of Animal Science collection. Used by permission.

146. ©2012 Helen Scanlon

INDEX

A

Abbott 9–12, 23–26
Ameer, Kari 98–100, 144–146
American Morgan Horse Association iv, 25–26, 91, 144–146
Anna Darling 44–45
awards
  Champion Classic Pleasure Saddle 73
  Champion Park Harness 41
  Champion Park Saddle Horse 86–87
  Champion, Road Hack 70–71
  Classic Pleasure Driving Champion 73
  Classic Pleasure Junior 73
  Classic Pleasure Saddle Reserve Champion 73
  Connecticut Morgan Horse Association Hall of Fame 56–58
  Eastern Grand Champion Stallion 46–47
  English Championship 78–79
  English Pleasure Amateur Class 70–71
  English Pleasure Championship 99–100
  English Pleasure World Champion 81
  Filly Foal Class 71
  First Place In-Hand 109–111
  Gold Cup Reserve Jr. Park Saddle Stallion 60
  Grand Champion In-Hand 86–87
  Grand Champion Stallion 41, 46–47, 90
  Grand Champion stallion in Pleasure Driving 67–69
  High Point Dressage Champions 21
  High Point Stallion 90
  Indy 500 Jr. Park Saddle Championship 60
  Jumper Championship 92
  Junior Champion 89–90, 94–95
  Low Hunter Champion 55–58
  Mare and Foal Class 82–85
  Morgan Horse of the Year 44–45
  National Champion 32–33, 35–36, 36, 44–45, 76–77
  National Morgan Horse Show 38–39, 76–77, 79
  Park Harness Champion 86–87
  Rafferty Challenge for Morgans 27
  Reserve Champion 33, 70–71, 73, 76–77, 78–79, 97, 101–104, 112
  Reserve Champion Classic Pleasure Saddle 73
  Reserve Champion for in-hand 33
  Reserve Champion in Carriage Driving 112

Reserve Champion in the English Pleasure 78–79
Reserve Champion Mare 76–77, 97
Reserve Champion Open Working Hunter 101–104
Reserve Champion, Road Hack 70, 70–71
Reserve Grand Champion 89
Reserve Grand National Mare 82–85
Reserve High Point Stallion 90
Reserve Junior Champion 89–90
Reserve World Champion Working Hunter 55
Road Hack Champion 55–58
USEF National Horse of the Year Morgan Carriage Champion 55–58
World Champion English Pleasure 52
World Champion Equitation Mount 55–58
World Champion Gelding 55–58
World Champion Working Hunter 55–58
World Champion yearling filly 121–122

B

Babbitt, Lynn 99–100, 144–146
Backs, Jennifer (*née* Gregson) 99–100, 144–146
Balch, Donald, Dr. 46–47, 144–146
Battell, Joseph, Colonel 6–7
Beckley, Leo 36
Bennett, John Jr. iv, 56–58, 61–63, 64–65, 67–69, 70–71, 72–73, 92, 102–104, 105, 112, 113,
        114–116, 117–120, 144–146
Bennfield 27
Bennfield's Ace 27
Bennington 7, 27
Biron, Julie 109–111, 118–120, 144–146
Blatt, Theresa 88, 144–146
Bobb, Arlis 13–21, 144–146
Brauch, Megan (*née* Heffley) 13–21, 114–116, 144–146
broodmare 76–77, 78–79, 80, 81, 82–85, 86–87, 88, 89–90, 91, 92, 94–95, 96, 98–100,
        101–104, 105, 106, 107–108, 109–111, 112, 114–118, 117–120, 121–122
Brooks, Bob 40–41, 42–43, 144–146
Budris, Timothy 102–104, 144–146
Busmich, Sandra, Dr. 101–104

C

Cade 2–4
Callahan, Janice 67–69, 88, 96, 101–104, 106, 109–111, 122, 144–146
Canfield 7, 27, 28, 35–36, 82–85
Carter, Andy 25–26, 29, 125–126
Chantwood Command 60

Chapman, Megan. *See* Thompson
Clark, Peggy 89–90, 121–122
Coats, Roy and Janie 87, 89–90
Connolly, Adelaide 125–126
Cowan, William Allen, Professor i–ii, 10–12, 24–26, 35–36, 38–39, 42–43, 48–58, 76–77,
      86–87, 91, 94–95, 97, 144–146
Crawford, Bill 44–45
Crawford, Lloyd 64–65, 144–146

D

Daughter of Diamond 2–4
Davis, Steve 144–146
Davis, Ted 38–39
Delmaytion Desire 101–104
DeWet, Patti 49–58
Dinger, James, Professor 91, 105, 144–146
Dragon 8–12
Dragon, Jr. 8–12

E

equestrian disciplines 8
   dressage 4, 11–12, 21, 99–100, 115–116
   Drill Team 67–69, 81, 101–104, 107–108, 121–122, 129
   English Pleasure 52–58, 70–71, 78–79, 81, 99–100
   Equestrian Team 109–111
   harness 40–41, 63
   In-Hand 44–45, 84–85, 86–87, 87, 109–111, 129
   Park 40–41, 41, 42–43, 44–45, 60, 84–85, 86–87, 87
   Pleasure Driving 67–69, 73, 84–85
   Pleasure Saddle 70–71, 73
   Road Hack 55–58, 70–71
   saddleseat 4, 33, 40–41, 68–69
   Western 30–31, 78–79, 84–85, 109–111
Evans, Robert 2–4

F

Fairytop 32–33
Ferguson, Cecil, J. 35–36
Figure 2–4, 6–7, 10–12, 32–33
Forst, Pat 84–85, 144–146

G

Gagnon, Jaclyn (*née* Gallant) 118–121, 144–146
Gallant, Jaclyn. *See* Gagnon
Garrigus, Harry L., Professor 9–12, 23–26
General Gates 6–7
Gibson, Murray 121–122
Glenney, Shirley 32–33, 144–146
Goldfield 27, 29, 30–31, 32–33
Greenwalt, Helen 79
Greenwalt, Richard and Irene 37
Gregson, Jennifer. *See* Backs

H

Haas, Richard and Andrea 51–58
Hale, Nathan, Professor 9–12, 48–58, 84–85, 144–146
Hartley, Harry 62, 92
Heffley, Megan. *See* Brauch
Henninger, Courtnay *See* Lawrence
Herd Sire 23–26, 27, 29, 30–31, 32–33, 35–36, 37, 38–39, 40–41, 42–43, 44–45, 46–47, 48–58, 60, 61–63, 64–65, 66–69

I

Intrepid Sovereign 41

J

Joyous 23–26
Juno 29

K

Kays, John, Professor 37
King, Daniel 68–69

L

Lawrence, Courtnay (*née* Henninger) 68–69, 98–100
Ledgemere Bounty 42–43, 98–100, 113
Lewis, Caitlin 70–71
Lussier, Jade 66–69, 144–146

Lydon, John 48–58

M

Magellan 29, 30–31
Mansfield 7, 27, 29
Mentor v–vii, 10–12, 29, 32–33, 35–36, 76–77, 79, 82–85
Merwin Black Beauty 97
Meyer, Kayleigh 72–73, 144–146
Military 5–7, 30 31
Morgan
  breed ii, iv, v–vii, 2–4, 5–7, 8–12, 13–21, 23–26, 27, 29, 30–31, 32–33, 36, 37, 38–39,
      40–41, 42–43, 44–45, 46–47, 48–58, 61–63, 64–65, 67–69, 70–71, 72–73, 75, 76–77,
      78–79, 82–85, 86–87, 88, 89–90, 91, 92, 94–95, 96, 97, 99–100, 101–104, 106,
      109–110, 112, 114–116, 118–120, 121–122, 128, 129, 131–143
  Justin 2–4
Mrs. Culvers 7

N

New England Morgan Horse Association (NEMHA) 35–36, 86–87, 89–90, 94–95
Noiles, Esther, Dr. 96, 105, 144–146
Noontide 10–12

O

O'Donovan, Mary 61–63, 107–108, 114–116, 144–146
Orcland John Darling 44–45, 45, 81
Orcutt, Lyman, Dr., and Cheryl 44–45, 48–58, 49–58, 50–58, 51–58, 56–58, 144–146
Owen, Mabel 86–87

P

Panfield ii, 7, 27, 35–36, 76–77, 78–79, 80, 81, 86–87, 89–90, 94–95
Parker, Leslie "Les" 51–58
Pelletier, Courtney 107–108, 122
Pelletier, Kathy 12, 60, 61–65, 67–69, 97, 107–108, 118–120, 122, 144–146
Pennsy 30–31, 32–33
Penny Royal 30–31
Perry, Arthur, Jr. 41, 144–146
Phillipa 23–26, 82–85

Q

Quakerlady 10–12, 32–33
Queen Wolfington 8–12
Quotation 32–33

R

Raven, Howard 23–26
Rienzi 5–7
Riviera 32–33
Rossi, David, Dr. 64–65, 144–146
Roto, Linda 113, 144–146
Royalanne 30–31

S

Salem Sentana 89–90, 106, 107–108, 121–122
Sentana 78–79, 80, 89–90, 106, 107–108, 121–122
Shaw, Johanna, Dr. 97
Sheba 32–33, 76–77, 78–79, 81, 86–87, 94–95
Sheridan, Philip, General 5–7
Shoe. *See* UC High Hopes
Song of Courage 106, 113–115
Stemmons, Walter 9–12
Stormin' Norman. *See* UC High Hopes

T

The Explorer 37, 82–85, 88
Theis, Locke 35–36
The Morgan Mile 3–4
Thompson, Megan (*née* Chapman) 101–104, 144–146
Tomastik, Nancy 114–116, 144–146
True Briton 2–4
Tsui, P.C., Major General 30–31

U

UC Acrobat 45, 94–95
UC Allegro 81
UC Applause 110–111
UC Archer 45
UC Aria 70–71, 107–108
UC Ariel 107–108
UC Aries 107–108

UC Arthur L 64–65, 102–104
UC Athena 88
UC Biz E Flirting 64–65
UC Blackberry 112
UC Black Razberry 112
UC Braveheart 68–69
UC Buckingham 97
UC Cadberry 68–69, 112
UC Cannie 23–26, 40–41, 82–85, 88
UC Carberry 112, 113
UC Carillion 45
UC Centerfold 97
UC Cinnamon 47
UC City Lights 92
UC Concertina 81, 92, 93
UC Conquistador 33
UC Contessa 82–85, 87
UC Cornucopia 88
UC Courage Under Fire 68–69, 106
UC Crackerjack 89–90
UC Crescendo 107–108
UC Curtain Call 102–104
UC Danegeld 47
UC Dark Shadow 39, 86–87
UC Desiree 60
UC Doc Daniels 13–21, 61–63, 70–71, 72–73, 97, 113
UC Doc Sanchez 72–73, 106, 113
UC Doc's Image 97
UC Domination 70–71, 107–108, 113
UC Donation 39, 80, 113
UC Ecstasy 37
UC Electra 41, 82–85, 87, 96, 105
UC Emma 110
UC Esther 105
UC Exhilaration 37
UC Expectation 37, 82–85, 88
UC Exploration 37
UC Expression 37
UC Fancy Bizness 64–65
UC Fascination 39, 48–58, 66–69, 80, 91, 119–120
UC Finale 77
UC First Edition 47
UC Flirtation 39, 80
UC Harmony 76–77
UC Harry H 92
UC Harvestor 43
UC Heather 76–77
UC High Hopes vii, 13–21, 116
UC Highlife 32–33

165

UC Holiday 91, 117–120
UC Hope and Courage 13–21, 67–69, 106, 114–116
UC Hopeful 45
UC Huckleberry 112
UC Irish Rhapsody 105
UC Justa Flirt 60
UC Kiwi 97
UC Last Tango 102–104
UC Legacy 83–85
UC Leonardo 68–69
UC Leprechaun 47
UC Lyre 107–108
UC Lyric 39, 48–58, 64–65, 81, 91, 94–95, 107–108
UC Marquis 39, 40–41, 82–85, 87, 96
UC Mastermind 74
UC Mayberry 112
UC Mayphil 23–26, 30–31
UC Melodie 36, 76–77, 81, 92, 94–95
UC Merlin 55–58, 91
UC Midnight Lace 97
UC Mischief Managed 71
UC Moonshadow 68–69, 112
UC Mr. T's Destiny 107–108
UC Olympic Star 107–108
UC Ovation 98–100, 109–111
UC Pandora 33
UC Pantana 78–79
UC Peppermint 47
UC Phoebe 97
UC Predictor 88
UC Prima Dona 39, 86–87
UC Reverie 76–77
UC Rhapsody 36, 76–77, 86–87, 96
UC Rianna 55–58
UC Ringmaster i–ii, vi–vii, 39, 48–58, 59, 64–65, 72–73, 74, 91, 94–95, 97, 102–104, 117–120
UC Rogue 14–21
UC Royal Dutchess 39
UC Senator 32–33, 79
UC Sensation 36, 79, 80, 91
UC Serenade 76–77
UC Serendipity 55–58, 101–104
UC Show Biz 64–65
UC Show Girl 64–65
UC Sonata 43, 94, 94–95, 98–100, 109–111, 122
UC Spicy Lass 41
UC Spring Break 64–65
UC Stanza 47
UC Sundance 97
UC Taffy 79, 89–90, 106, 120–122

UC Tee Rose 55–58
UC Tee Time 67–69, 72–73, 106
UC Three Times a Lady 105
UC Tip Top 43
UC Topaz 43, 61–63, 112, 113
UC Top Brass 55–58, 91
UC Top Hat 55–58
UC Toronado 13–21, 66–69, 91, 105, 112, 114–116
UC Town Crier 55–58, 102–104
UC Traveler 81
UC Valhalla 47
UC Wilde Mark 55–58, 91, 118–120
Ulendon 44–45
United States Government iv, 5–7, 9–12
  cavalry 5–7, 10–12, 13–21, 31, 52–58
  Government Horse Farm 5–7, 9–12, 23–26, 27, 29, 30–31, 32–33, 35–36
University of Connecticut i–ii, iv, v–vii, 7, 8–12, 13–21, 23–27, 29, 30–33, 35–37, 38–47,
    48–58, 60, 61–74, 76–92, 94–95, 96, 97, 98–100, 101–104, 105, 106, 107–108,
    109–111, 113–120, 121–122, 125–129, 131–148
  College of Agriculture and Natural Resources Department of Animal Science i–ii, vii,
    9–12, 24–26, 37, 48–58, 61–63, 83–85
  Connecticut Agricultural College 8–12, 23–26
  Connecticut State College 9–12, 125–126
  Equine Program i–ii, 11–12, 82–85
Upwey Ben Don 35–36, 38–39, 40–41, 46–47, 60, 94–95
UVM Viking 46–47

W

Walters, Bruce 49–58, 83–85, 126
Wang, S.C., Major General 30–31
war 5–7, 13–21, 31, 38–39
Waseeka's Showtime 48–58, 64–65, 91
Wiktor, Anne 83–85, 85, 144–146
Windcrest Don Again 38–39, 40–41, 76–77, 80, 81, 82–85, 86–87, 89–90, 91, 92, 94–95
Wood, J. Harry 78–79

Made in the USA
Charleston, SC
14 September 2013